NORSE MAGIK
ODIN AND THOR

David Thompson

NORSE MAGIK
ODIN AND THOR

David Thompson

TRANS MUNDANE
PUBLISHING
OCCULT KNOWLEDGE

To The Nine

A Warning:

This is very powerful material. When worked properly, you may see unexpected results. These rituals and petitions are like electricity, the energy will flow in the direction of the intended output. In saying this, please be firm in your intentions and make absolutely sure what you want is truly want you desire.

As they say, be careful what you wish for, you just might get it.

Hello!

For you, this might be the first book on magik, or the first book on MY magik you are reading. I strive to make this as accessible as possible for people new to Magik.

Many readers may not know this, but I do not tend to "blow my own horn," so I don't market my services like I should. On the advice of multiple people, I'm including this brief "horn blowing" in all new books.

I have a modest website: https://davepsychic.com

Everyone sometimes has trouble making their magik work. To that, I offer ritual services, I also do readings and attunements, and I'm considering some protection, removal services. Most dark/black entities are connected to larger black systems, and it can take a bit to cast them away.

I also offer one-on-one workings, which is an educational program. I can teach you based upon your level, and I expect you to actually take part in the exercises.

Check it out. I also have a contact page, but it might take me a few days to answer due to the volume of emails I get daily.

I also have a teaching website - https://highmagikacademy.com

This is where one can enroll in any of my classes. Videos and handouts for each class.

PREFACE

(Just a piece of fiction I wrote a while back, when I was looking at a series about the Norse.)

Skaal trudged through the muck. The slippery mud proved even more slippery as he approached the small village where he hoped to find a sympathetic ear.

Skaal had a problem. A big problem. A problem involving his warrior wife and a newly acquired slave. Skaal had returned from a raid of the west islands and had dragged a strapping young man to help with the small farm and tend to the herd of cattle.

Instead, after another raiding trip, Skaal had found the farm abandoned. Fearing the worse, he asked around and found out that no; it wasn't a raiding party from a rival tribe, but his wife had decided to run away with the slave.

So, the cuckolded Viking had now hiked miles across muddy trails and roads, hoping to find a village's volva, a magic worker, to help him petition Odin for the return of his wife. The slave could stay away, as far as he was concerned. At least, find a volva who wouldn't shake her head in laughter.

Skaal wasn't the brightest of men, but he was a great warrior. Yet, no matter how mighty his deeds in a raid, he still could not get the cows or sheep on his farm to make more animals.

After explaining why he needed his wife to return, the last village's volva laughed hard enough to almost black out due to a lack of oxygen. In between bouts of laughter, that village's volva had tried to question the man on how he expected to satisfy his wife if he did not know what he was doing, which also included the farm animals, why should his wife return?

Finally, after a week of hiking, Skaal arrived in a larger village, and he stopped to glance around. A figure appeared, almost as if out of mist, by the closed door to a smaller longhouse. The figure approached Skaal. Temped to flee, the laugher from the last village still burning his ears, he stood his ground as the figure approached.

The figure stopped and faced Skaal. Hands pulled away the hood, revealing an older woman with streaks of silver in her hair, which was braided into what appeared to be serpents around her head.

Skaal started to speak, but the woman pressed a hand firmly against his mouth.

"Speak not," she said, firmly. Her accent was difficult for Skaal, but he understood the gesture. "You are filthy. You will not step foot into my room until you bathe and clean your clothing."

She stepped back and waved one hand. Two young girls came running, and they each took a hand and led Skaal away.

As he was dragged away, protesting that he wasn't all that dirty, the old woman sighed. She turned as another figure walked up.

"Is that man your husband?" the Volva asked.

"Yes." The other woman was tall, dressed for battle, with her head half shaved, ready for a raiding voyage. Kara.

"He hasn't even once — ?" the older woman made a rude gesture with her body, thrusting her hips forward.

"He can't locate his cock with both hands and a guide!" Kara spit out. "How could he have found me here?"

"He has wandered aimlessly. He was not tracking you. What do you wish done?"

"Send him on a long quest. Make up something. Something dangerous. So that he disappears. I plan to set out tomorrow and ransom that young man, or maybe marry him."

"You could do both. Ransom him, then lure him away," the Volva said, looking up at the striking woman. "But only if you can keep that boy addled by your talents."

Skaal's protests about bathing could be heard all across the village. "I only married the idiot because his father is Jarl, and I was promised a boat and crew for myself."

"I'd think he had other sons that you could have married," the older woman mused.

"Just daughters. He was cursed with daughters," Kara growled.

INTRODUCTION

Welcome to my book on Norse Magik!

Perhaps, like any other child from my era, I was fascinated by the Vikings. Only later did I know these people by their actual name, the Norse. Well, actually, ancient people from the area known as Scandinavia. According to the internet, this is a subregion of Northern Europe, with strong historical, cultural, and linguistic ties between its constituent peoples. Scandinavia most commonly refers to Denmark, Norway, and Sweden. It can sometimes also refer to the Scandinavian Peninsula.

It was more than I cared to learn when I was pushing toy longboats across the floor or subjecting the brave Vikings in these boats to torturous sea conditions. Meaning I played with them in the bathtub, causing water to slosh out and onto the floor. Later, my mother would ask if I had managed to get ALL the water out of the tub and onto the floor. Well, not for a lack of trying.

Now, Norse magik. This is actually my second book on this, the first being Freya and Frigg, but it's in a different series, and I'm a bit too lazy to change that.

In this book, I'll only look at Odin and Thor. And not the characters found in the modern movies. These deities are not comic book characters. They're serious deities, and as such, deserve a serious look.

This book is organized into two main parts, each beginning with a brief historical overview of the myths and magik, followed by how this magik can be applied to modern ritual methods.

Norse mythology is fascinating, and the magik that Odin or Thor can bring to your magik practice is strong and easily accessed. That is, once you get to the root of the magik itself, and then listen to the deities as they explain how they wish to be approached and petitioned.

My method strips the traditional Norse magik of the archaic trappings and blocks put in place by the "gatekeepers" of magik. You've probably encountered this type—the person who claims one is guilty of cultural appropriation, that one must do specific tasks prior to working this magik, that outdated cultural trappings are necessary, or even that these deities are just too busy to deal with inferior mortals.

To that, I usually say, "Ah, to hell with you." (Actually, I use a much stronger phrase, but I'll let your imagination run wild with what it is.)

I loathe gatekeepers. Briefly, these are individuals or groups who act as self-appointed "guardians" of certain knowledge, practices, or traditions. These people often claim that only they, or those who follow their specific rules, are "allowed" to access or practice magik effectively. They may dismiss others' approaches, criticize newer interpretations, or make people feel unworthy unless they meet arbitrary standards.

Gatekeeping stifles exploration, creativity, and personal connection to magik. Magik is deeply personal and evolves with the practitioner. While learning from tradition is valuable, no one owns the path to spiritual or magikal growth—it's a journey that belongs to each of us.

A whole lot of nonsense. As humans, if we get a traditional upbringing, we're taught that we're not anywhere near the "level" of these mysterious beings and certainly not worthy of even talking directly to them.

A good example is one individual I encountered several years ago. This person claimed to be the only one who could control specific spirits and insisted that only by following their way could anyone ever achieve success as magicians. Upon meeting this person, I thought to myself, "I'll avoid the holiday rush and start loathing this jerk now." Enormous ego. Expecting everyone to do the work for them. Yeah, that person.

Fast forward, and they got what usually happens to the most vile cult leaders—they lost their following when it was revealed that the "special entity" they were making people "feed" was actually a dark, lower-dimensional being that had this person firmly in its grasp.

Yeah.

Okay, I'll climb down off my podium.

My Magik Method

Simplicity. Available to anyone. Easily used by anyone.

Not a lot of claptrap. (A phrase we don't use near enough anymore.)

I use a template for presenting the rituals. I'll first cover the usual items called for in a ritual, then I'll present my version, which works so much faster and better.

Magik, mine or anyone else's, comes down to intent. That's it. As simple as that. Your intent determines the success or failure of your magik.

If you have unclear goals—illustrated by filling the petition with all sorts of nonessential terms, asking for the magik to deliver in an overly specific manner, or dictating an arbitrary deadline—it will hinder the magik.

Nothing stops magik as fast as a deadline—except trying to dictate exactly how it must unfold.

Years ago, I had a client contact me, begging me to drop everything and help. Then this person demanded the magik work in a specific way, and by a very definite date. Of course, their magik failed. So, they turned to me, and I had to explain that magik simply doesn't work in this manner.

Yes, I do assist people in making magik happen, but when one demands the magik occur by a set time or date, I will refuse the booking and refund the fee. That is the biggest reason anyone's magik fails. Following that is restricting how the magik is supposed to work. For example, a client told me to make sure the person who owed a specific debt paid on their own and not be forced. I advised against this. I said that by this point, this person wasn't going to repay them and needed to be forced.

So, my magik method is one where you do not need archaic rituals, exotic offerings, bizarre incense, or ritual props. I usually specify a certain color of candle, but even this takes a back seat to your intent. Take any color candle and light it with intent, and it'll work magik. Write a simple petition, generate a simple sigil, and the magik happens.

Your desire manifests.

As an example, I have been wanting to make astronomical images since I was a teenager. I would strap my old film camera to the telescope mount, a simple clockwork motor that would sorta keep an object in the telescope's field of view. I'd look at the pictures in books, and I wanted to do that.

It was quite difficult in the 1970s. Film just wasn't made for long exposures of a deep-space object, and it took hours of exposure time, and the telescope mount simply wasn't good enough. In college, I got to use a bigger telescope—an enormous device built in the early 1910s. Yet, I wasn't able to get what I wanted.

Now, fast forward several decades, and I'm in an area with fairly dark skies—when it isn't cloudy—and I have attempted to get some images. The nebula in Orion, mostly. So, I simply "wanted." I threw intent behind a few candles. That was it. I didn't petition any deity, no tedious meditation. I just decided that was what I was going to get.

Now, if you follow me on social media (links at the back of this book), you'll see I have now accomplished what I wanted to do in the 1970s. The first images I got were of the galaxy known as Andromeda. It took some bucks in equipment, including a PC powerful enough to process hundreds of images into a single final image. The money simply was there to be used for this. All my needs were easily met, with a hefty surplus.

That is the power of intent.

What does this have to do with Odin and Thor?

Not a lot. Honestly. It's just one of those personal anecdotes to prove a point that intent, and only intent, can manifest a desire.

Add onto that, asking a deity/entity/spirit nicely to help will accomplish amazing manifestations in your life. The biggest obstacle is your belief in yourself and your magik.

The Summoning and Sigils

The two are tied intimately in this book. Simply holding the sigil of Odin makes the psychic connection to the spirit you wish to summon. Then, all it takes is to ask that they join with you. No lengthy phrases to speak, just straight into the magik.

Understanding the Basics of Norse Magik

This book is about Norse Magik, so let's take a quick look at the basics before diving into the aspects and magik of Mister Wednesday and his easily angered son, Thor.

Most of what we know about the Norse pantheon wasn't written down until about 1300 A.D. Imagine that. This was after the area became Christianized. Before this, these stories were part of an oral tradition, passed down through generations by skalds (poets) and storytellers. During the dark winter months, the people would listen to these stories by the light of huge fires in the middle of the longhouse.

Understand this—Norse Magik isn't just about chanting spells or lighting candles. It's much more than that. Norse Magik is a living, breathing energy that connects you to ancient forces that still hum beneath the surface of our world today. Imagine standing under a sky filled with stars, the northern lights flickering in an otherworldly dance, as if the gods themselves are painting messages across the heavens. That's the essence of Norse Magik—cosmic power, earthy roots, and the wisdom of ages.

I'm fortunate to live far enough north that the northern lights will sometimes extend to where I can see them. This past summer (2024), I witnessed an enormous aurora display—streamers of color spread across the entire sky. For most of the rest of the summer and into the late fall, the displays continued. It's a sight I'll not forget.

Norse Magik is not a singular system. It's a collection of practices evolved from the mythology, culture, and daily lives of the Norse people. Like with the Native American traditions in the United States, this magik is deeply tied to these people's understanding of the cosmos and their place within it. These guys were rugged and resilient, living close to nature in a world where survival wasn't guaranteed. If death didn't come from a wild animal or a storm at sea, it might come from warring neighbors—or even someone else in the village.

Magik was a tool—a way to align themselves with the forces of the universe. It was as much a part of their daily lives as it was their sacred rites. It was an everyday thing, worked by almost everyone. However, most villages had people who'd be more attuned to the ebb and flow of magik. They called these people "godi." Among them were Seidkona (female) and Seidman (male), as well as seeresses or prophetesses—women who often traveled between villages to share prophecies or messages from the gods.

They didn't see themselves as separate from the natural world or the divine. Instead, they acknowledged the interconnectedness of all things. To practice Norse Magik is to tap into that web of connection, to work with the energies flowing through the cosmos and within yourself.

Take, for example, Yggdrasil, the great World Tree. To the Norse, it wasn't just a tree; it was the spine of existence, its roots reaching deep into the unknown, its branches stretching into the divine. In the same way, Norse Magik connects the practitioner to the past, present, and future, grounding them in the here and now while opening pathways to the mysteries beyond.

One key concept in Norse Magik is Wyrd—the web of fate. Wyrd isn't just about destiny in the sense of a preordained future. Instead, it's a vast, interconnected tapestry of events, choices, and consequences. Think of it like a spider's web, with every action sending ripples through the entire structure. Understanding Wyrd means understanding that your actions matter—that every choice you make is a thread woven into the fabric of your life. In magik, this awareness gives you the power to influence your path, to pull on certain threads to shape your reality.

Wyrd is pronounced like "wurd" if you want to sound fancy—or a bit like a LARP nerd—but saying "weird" works just as well.

One facet of Norse Magik is its practical, no-nonsense approach. Like me, these folks weren't interested in complicated rituals for ceremony's sake. Their magik was straightforward, purposeful, and deeply tied to intention. Need protection? Carve runes on your shield. Need to ensure a good harvest? Offer to Freyr, the god of fertility and prosperity. Need guidance? Seek out Odin, who sacrificed himself for the wisdom of the runes. Their magik was grounded in necessity, and this grounding is what makes it so accessible and powerful today.

But don't mistake simplicity for lack of depth. Each symbol, each rune, each invocation carries layers of meaning. To work this Magik is to jump headfirst into a well of wisdom, where every drop holds stories, lessons, and power. For example, the rune Ansuz, associated with Odin, is more than just a symbol— it's a gateway to communication, inspiration, and divine connection. To trace it in the air or carve it into wood is to call upon the Allfather himself, to invite his energy into your workings.

While the Norse magicians of old might have worked their magik with bone tools and animal hides, the principles remain the same today. I'll tell you how to use a modern altar or an open patch of earth in the woods to work Norse Magik.

It's about intention, connection, and respect for the forces you're working with.

This isn't about mastering a set of rules; it's about understanding a way of being—walking through the world with an awareness of the magik in every stone, every gust of wind, and every whispered word from the gods. It's not something you do; it's something you live.

Don't worry if you can't find exactly what I recommend in this book. Find a substitute and keep on going. No green candles? Use white. It's that simple.

PART ONE

ODIN

CHAPTER 1

Aspects of Odin

Odin, the Allfather of the Norse pantheon, is a god of many faces. From the wise and enigmatic wanderer to the fierce and commanding warlord, his multifaceted nature reveals countless paths for spiritual and magikal connection. This chapter I'll cover Odin's rich mythology, his relentless quest for knowledge, and his deep connection to the runes, which he sacrificed much to obtain. By understanding these aspects, you'll uncover how Odin's energy can inspire transformation, wisdom, and power in your magik.

Odin is not just a god; he's an extremely complex being, an enigma wrapped in mystery, power, and wisdom, a figure whose many aspects can be as elusive as the winds themselves.

Think of him as the ultimate shape-shifter, not just in form but in function. Odin is a god of paradox—both a ruthless warrior and a deeply introspective philosopher, both a king and a wanderer. To understand Odin is to explore the very nature of transformation, the balance between destruction and creation, and the search for meaning in a chaotic world.

One of the most striking things about Odin is his ability to embody different roles, each one revealing another layer of his vast complexity. When you think of Odin, do you imagine the bearded, one-eyed god sitting upon his throne in Asgard, surveying all with a keen eye? That is certainly one of his aspects—the **Allfather**, the ruler of the **Aesir**, the god who commands respect and leads with unyielding authority. But this is just one face of Odin, the one that inspires reverence and awe.

Odin is also the **Wanderer**. This is where Odin's personality becomes more relatable, more human in its longing. He is the god who chooses to travel the nine realms, seeking knowledge at any cost, even if it means sacrificing a part of himself. Imagine setting out on a journey with nothing but your own wits and courage to guide you—no map, no destination, only the raw hunger for wisdom. That's Odin's path. His wanderings are a metaphor for our own search for understanding, and this is why he is so deeply connected to magik: he doesn't wait for knowledge to come to him, he seeks it relentlessly.

Another aspect of Odin—the **Seeker of Wisdom**—is

perhaps the most significant for users of Norse magik. It is this aspect that led him to sacrifice an eye at Mimir's well in exchange for wisdom that would help him navigate the chaos of the worlds. Think of this as a metaphor for the cost of true knowledge: sometimes, the price of understanding is steep. But for Odin, the pursuit of wisdom was worth any sacrifice, because wisdom is the key to wielding true power. Ask yourself, what you are willing to sacrifice for knowledge and power? Think on this before any workings to this aspect.

In addition to all his other attributes, Odin's character is also defined by his role as the God of War, another crucial element of his persona. But this isn't the brutal, mindless violence of a simple warrior—this is the god who strategizes, who leads battles with cunning and foresight. Odin's warriorship is not just about strength; it's about knowing when to fight and how to win. His warriors are not just brawn—they are carefully selected, like the Einherjar, the chosen dead who dine with him in Valhalla, preparing for the final battle of Ragnarok. If you think about Odin in this aspect, think of him as a general who understands the intricacies of war—the timing, the deception, the art of battle. It's about strategy and sacrifice, and it resonates deeply with anyone who seeks to win their own battles in life, whether physical, emotional, or spiritual.

Finally, there's the Odin of the Runes—the god who gave his own body to obtain the ancient knowledge of runes. The story of Odin hanging from Yggdrasil, pierced by his own spear, for nine days and nights in a self-imposed sacrifice, is not just myth; it's a powerful reminder of the lengths we must go to in our quest for true understanding. The runes are not just symbols—they are keys to unlocking the mysteries of the universe, and Odin himself is their master. To invoke Odin through the runes is to invite both wisdom and sacrifice into your life. It's a powerful act that taps into the very core of Norse magik.

Each of these aspects—Odin the Allfather, the Wanderer, the God of War, and the Master of Runes—offer unique energies and qualities to work with in magik. As you continue your journey through this book, you will learn to connect with these facets of Odin using his wisdom and strength to guide your own path. Odin is not a god you simply worship from afar. He is a presence that demands engagement, that challenges you to dig deep, to sacrifice, and to strive for greatness.

And that's what makes Odin such a fascinating and powerful figure in Norse magik. He is not just an idea, not just a symbol of power—he is an active, dynamic force, one that continues to shape the cosmos and all those who seek his knowledge. So, as you move forward in your exploration of Odin's magik, remember: the journey is just beginning, and the Allfather himself is waiting for you to ask the questions that will transform your world.

Modern Aspects of Odin

I'm going to quickly go over some common aspects of Odin. These are aspects I was able to glean from my contacts with Odin. These aspects are closely related to his mythological aspects, but when working this magik, one doesn't need to locate deer antlers and other Viking-era props.

Wisdom for Business Success and Strategic Thinking

Odin's relentless pursuit of knowledge makes him an invaluable ally in navigating the challenges of modern business. Whether you're seeking clarity on a career move, strategizing the launch of a new venture, or managing workplace conflicts, Odin's wisdom provides a powerful edge. He doesn't simply hand you the answers—he sharpens your instincts and opens your mind to new possibilities. Think of him as the ultimate strategist, whispering the kind of insights that help you see opportunities others overlook or plan ten steps ahead of your competition.

His energy teaches us that success often requires sacrifice and focus. Just as Odin sacrificed his eye at Mimir's Well to gain unmatched wisdom, working with him invites you to make the hard choices needed for growth. Perhaps it's letting go of a stagnant job or committing to an ambitious project you've been hesitant to pursue. Odin's guidance will push you to trust your abilities and act decisively, helping you unlock the path to success.

Finding Love and Connecting with Your Life Partner

In love, Odin's mastery of Wyrd—the Norse concept of fate—can align your life with someone whose thread is meant to weave with yours. This isn't about forcing love or manipulating others; it's about creating the conditions for authentic, meaningful connections. Odin's wisdom can help you recognize the right person when they appear or guide you toward experiences that bring your ideal partner into your life.

Working with Odin for love might feel unconventional at first. After all, he's not a deity typically associated with romance. But his ability to see the grand design of life makes him uniquely qualified to reveal the hidden patterns connecting you to others. If you're ready to find your life partner—or even strengthen an existing bond—calling on Odin can help you uncover what's needed to build a love that lasts.

Gaining Confidence and Authority

As the Allfather and leader of the Aesir, Odin embodies authority and influence. His energy can help you step into a leadership role, command respect, and project confidence in personal and professional situations. Whether you're presenting a bold idea at work, leading a team, or striving to make your voice heard, Odin's presence fortifies your ability to inspire and guide others.

Calling on Odin isn't just about outward displays of power; it's about cultivating inner confidence. He teaches that true authority begins with self-belief and clarity of purpose. When you work with him, you'll feel his energy reinforcing your strengths, helping you step into any room with a sense of control and assurance that others can't ignore.

Discovering Hidden Opportunities

Odin is a master of uncovering what lies beneath the surface, making him a powerful ally for finding opportunities where others see none. His ravens, Huginn (Thought) and Muninn (Memory), symbolize this gift, bringing knowledge from far and wide to those who call upon him. Whether it's a business deal you hadn't considered, a career opening you didn't notice, or even a chance encounter that changes everything, Odin's influence can illuminate paths you didn't know existed.

When you work with Odin for uncovering hidden opportunities, you'll notice subtle shifts—ideas bubbling up, coincidences that feel too perfect to be random, or a newfound ability to connect the dots between seemingly unrelated events. He sharpens your intuition and helps you tune into the possibilities all around you, even in the most unexpected places.

Transformation and Letting Go

Odin's story is one of transformation, often through great sacrifice. He teaches us that growth comes not from clinging to the past but from embracing change, even when it's uncomfortable. If you're starting over, facing a major transition, or needing to release old habits that no longer serve you, Odin's energy can help you move forward.

His sacrifices—his eye for wisdom, his time on Yggdrasil for the runes—are reminders that letting go of something valuable can lead to even greater rewards. Working with Odin for transformation means confronting what's holding you back and finding the courage to leave it behind. He doesn't promise an easy path, but he shows you that the journey is always worth it.

Creative Inspiration and Problem-Solving

Odin isn't just a warrior and ruler; he's also a poet and a creator. His influence is perfect for anyone seeking fresh ideas, whether you're working on a creative project, solving a tricky problem, or innovating in your field. He helps you see the world from new perspectives, sparking inspiration and encouraging bold thinking.

When you call on Odin for creativity, expect breakthroughs that seem to come from nowhere. A sudden idea, a solution that feels like it's been waiting for you to notice it, or a renewed sense of motivation to tackle challenges in inventive ways—all of these are his gifts. His energy is especially helpful when you're stuck, pushing you past blocks and into a flow of creativity.

Guidance in Life's Big Decisions

Life is full of crossroads, and making the right choice can feel overwhelming. This is where Odin's wisdom truly shines. He doesn't hand you a simple answer but helps you see the situation clearly, weigh your options, and trust your instincts. His presence is like having a wise mentor beside you, offering insight that cuts through doubt and confusion.

When you connect with Odin for guidance, you'll often find that his answers come in unexpected ways—a sudden realization, a vivid dream, or a moment of clarity when you least expect it. Trusting his process can lead you to decisions that align with your true path, even if they're not the ones you initially imagined.

These aspects of Odin's power—focused on business, love, leadership, creativity, and personal growth—are not relics of an ancient past. They are as practical and transformative today as they were for the Norse people, helping you tackle modern challenges with wisdom and strength. Through the rituals and guidance in this book, you'll discover how to bring Odin's energy into your own life and let his timeless wisdom illuminate your path forward.

CHAPTER 2

Ancient Magik with Odin

When fitting Odin into my style of magik, I found myself in the presence of an old-fashioned deity spirit. His suggestions all seemed to push this book toward traditional Norse magik.

So, I disconnected and looked for an alternative path—a mode of magik that is useful, simple, and effective. I reconnected with Odin's energy and peered deeply into this cold, solid block of power that everyone calls the Allfather.

He resists.

Because of this, I'll present a traditional ritual that will work for asking Odin to join you. Take note: you'll need to find some specific props for this type of ritual.

After this ritual template, we'll dive into a more familiar

ritual template.

Preparation

Some props you're going to need (some of these we'll use in the other rituals):

Candles

White, gray, or blue candles to represent wisdom, clarity, and Odin's connection to the divine

and cosmic knowledge.

Offering Bowl

A simple wooden or metal bowl for offerings, reflecting the practical tools of the Norse people.

Offerings

Mead (traditional honey wine) or ale as the most appropriate offerings, as they were commonly

given in Norse rituals. Bread or dried fish can also be used.

Alternatively, incense like frankincense or cedar can serve as a symbolic offering.

Symbol of Odin

A rune, such as Ansuz (associated with communication and wisdom) or Othala (ancestral

knowledge), carved into wood or stone.

A small replica of a spear (symbolizing Gungnir) or a representation of ravens or wolves.

Runes or Rune Set

A set of runes for divination or to use as a focus during the ritual, reflecting Odin's mastery of

runes.

Feathers or Animal Symbols

Black feathers to symbolize Huginn and Muninn (Thought and Memory).

Wolf imagery, to honor Geri and Freki, Odin's loyal companions.

Staff or Wand

A simple wooden staff or wand to represent Odin's role as a wanderer and guide.

Circle-Casting Materials

Stones, branches, or symbolic representations of the Nine Worlds to outline the sacred space.

Altar Cloth or Surface

Use a natural material, such as linen or wool, as the base for your ritual space. Traditional

Norse rituals were often simple, so a rustic, natural aesthetic fits well.

Lighting

A single oil lamp or torch to symbolize Odin's eternal wisdom, though modern practitioners

often use candles.

Knife or Ritual Blade

A knife (blótspjót) for cutting herbs, carving runes, or

symbolically "sacrificing" energy. Note:

This is symbolic and not used for harm.

Optional Additions

Tree Symbolism: A branch or small piece of wood to represent Yggdrasil, the World Tree.

Animal Tokens: If possible, representations of ravens, wolves, or a horse (Sleipnir).

Herbs: Sage, mugwort, or juniper for purification or to burn as incense.

Mead Horn or Drinking Vessel: A horn or cup for offering and toasting Odin.

When I was running a test ritual, to see how things flowed, I did not have either mead or a true ale on hand. I grabbed an old can of beer, an IPA (India Pale Ale) and figured to use that. It was left in my refrigerator after a large family dinner I'd hosted in November. Once in the ritual, with Odin pressing in at me, I picked up the can, opened it and poured a sizable portion into a goblet.

I heard, very plainly, *"What, in my name, are you offering me?"*

In the dim candlelight, I peered at the can and read the label more carefully. It was a **non-alcoholic, gluten-free beer.**

The silence from Odin was heavy.

I apologized and reached for a bottle of scotch.

This next section is unique. I went into a deep trance, and sat with Odin, and asked him questions, which he answered using "automatic writing". These are HIS answers.

An Interview with Odin

Question 1: What created you?

Ah, that is a question befitting a seeker of knowledge. What created me? The answer is not so simple, for I am both born and self-made. My origins lie in the vast void before creation, the Ginnungagap, where fire met ice, and the worlds began to take shape. I am a son of Borr and Bestla, their blood coursing through my veins, but my true essence? That I forged myself through relentless pursuit, sacrifice, and will.

I was shaped by the primordial forces, yes, but it was my thirst for wisdom that truly gave me form. When I hung from Yggdrasil, sacrificing myself to myself, I was reborn as more than just a god—I became a force of transformation. Creation is not a singular event but an ongoing process, and I am its living embodiment. I am the creator and the created, as all who seek knowledge must be.

Question 2: What are your likes, and what do you want to see in an old-fashioned ritual?

I have a fondness for offerings that are given with intent and respect. Mead, of course, is my drink of choice. The golden liquid carries more than taste—it carries history, tradition, and the warmth of camaraderie. A horn of mead raised in my honor pleases me greatly. Bread, fish, or even meat roasted over a fire are fitting, but it is the spirit of the offering that matters most. A simple bowl of clean water offered with sincerity can speak louder than grand feasts served without care.

In an old-fashioned ritual, I would see fire—a flame that burns brightly, symbolizing knowledge and the spark of the divine. I enjoy the sound of your voice, whether through poetry, song, or invocation. The words matter, yes, but more so the feeling behind them. Speak from the heart, and I will listen.

Symbols are powerful and should not be overlooked. Runes carved into wood, etched in stone, or drawn upon parchment call to me. My spear, Gungnir, is a sacred representation of my will and focus, and its image strengthens the connection. Feathers, to honor my ravens Huginn and Muninn, and tokens of wolves, for Geri and Freki, also call to me.

What I do not care for are empty gestures. A ritual that is performed as if it were a chore, without understanding or intent, is hollow. If you honor me, do so with thought and purpose, even if the ritual is simple.

Question 3: How do you want people in the here and now to approach you, how to summon you, and what offerings do you want from currently available items?

In the here and now, approach me with honesty. I see through falsehoods and half-measures. Do not fear me, but do not take me lightly. When you seek me, be prepared to act on what I reveal, for wisdom is wasted on those who do not use it. I do not demand perfection, but I do demand effort.

To summon me, create a space of intention. Light a candle, let its flame represent the spark of your will, and speak my name. Call me as the Allfather, the Wanderer, or the Seeker of Runes—titles hold power, and the one you use will shape how I answer. Speak your request clearly, for I do not care for riddles from mortals; I leave those for myself.

Offerings in this age need not be elaborate, but they must carry meaning. Mead, if you have it, pleases me greatly, but wine, beer, or even clear water given with respect suffices. Write your questions or desires on paper, burn them in my honor, and let the smoke carry them to me. Feathers, stones, or small carvings of runes make excellent tributes.

I care not for the grandness of the ritual or the rarity of the items; I care for the intent behind them. A sincere whisper in the night, a flame lit in quiet devotion, or a simple act of remembrance can call me. Approach me as a seeker, with courage in your heart and respect in your soul, and you will find that I am never far.

Question 4: How Did You Devise the Runes, and How Did You Teach Them to Humans?

Ah, the runes. They are not merely symbols etched in stone or wood—they are the secrets of existence, the threads that bind the worlds together. They are older than gods and men, older even than the roots of Yggdrasil, yet it was I who brought their power into the light and made them known to those bold enough to seek them.

How did I devise the runes, you ask? I did not so much create them as uncover them. They were always there, hidden in the fabric of the cosmos, waiting to be grasped by a will strong enough and a mind sharp enough to understand their meaning. That was the challenge. To gain their wisdom, I had to make a sacrifice, one so profound it nearly unmade me.

I hung from Yggdrasil, the great World Tree, for nine nights and nine days, pierced by my own spear, Gungnir. No food, no drink, nothing but the howling winds and the weight of my purpose to keep me company. I dangled between life and death, between this world and the other, staring into the void where the runes waited. Each night, I felt myself unraveling, and with each dawn, I came closer to grasping their truths. On the ninth night, the runes revealed themselves to me—not as mere marks, but as living forces. They burned into my mind, into my very being, and I understood.

I saw the power they held: the ability to shape thought, destiny, and reality itself. They were not gifts; they were a burden, a responsibility. To wield the runes was to wield creation and destruction, wisdom and folly. Their knowledge demanded a price, and I paid it with my blood, my pain, and my very self.

When I returned, I did not hoard the runes for myself. No, their power was too vast, too important to be locked away. I taught them to humankind, but not freely. The runes are not a treasure to be given lightly. Only those with the courage to seek them, the discipline to learn them, and the wisdom to use them were worthy of their secrets.

I shared the runes with the seers, the warriors, the poets, and the healers—each finding in them the truths they sought. To the seers, the runes became a way to divine the threads of fate. To the warriors, they offered protection and strength in battle. The poets found inspiration and the ability to weave words with power, while the healers uncovered their use in restoring balance to body and spirit. The runes, you see, are as versatile as they are profound.

Yet, I did not teach them in full to anyone. Each rune holds layers of meaning, and even now, I reveal only what a seeker is ready to understand. Some meanings are simple, practical. Others are cosmic, elusive, understood only by those who walk the shadowed paths of wisdom. This is their nature, and it is why they endure.

So, you ask how I taught the runes to humans? I taught them through experience, through trial, and through silence. For every answer I gave, I left a question unanswered. For every rune I explained, I left its deeper meaning for the seeker to uncover. The runes are a mirror, reflecting what is within you, and they will reveal themselves in full only when you are ready to bear their weight.

To this day, the runes remain my gift to humankind. A gift that comes with a challenge: to seek, to learn, to grow. Use them well, and they will serve you. Misuse them, and they will unravel you as surely as they once tested me. That is the nature of their power.

And finally, I asked about the old rituals to summon him. Here's the answer:

The Old Ritual to Summon Me, as Told by Odin

The rituals of old were not bound by excess or unnecessary pomp; they were born of necessity and woven with intent. If you sought me in the days of your ancestors, you would first prepare a sacred space—a clearing in the woods, perhaps, or the heart of a great hall. The place mattered less than the reverence carried in your heart, though it was often a space connected to the natural world, as Yggdrasil binds all things together.

The Sacred Fire

A fire would be lit, always central, always alive. Its flame was not just warmth but a symbol of connection between the worlds—Midgard where you stood, Asgard where I reside, and the unseen places in between. The fire was the axis, much like the World Tree itself, and it carried your words upward, your smoke rising like whispers to my ears.

The Offering

Ah, the offering—this was where intent was most clearly shown. Mead, golden and fragrant, was often poured onto the ground or into an offering bowl. Meat or bread, sometimes a portion of a hunt or the best of a harvest, would be placed near the fire, the smoke carrying the essence to me. Occasionally, sacrifices were made, not in cruelty but in recognition of the cost of asking the gods for their favor. A portion of what was given to you was offered back to the forces that sustain you.

The Words

You would then speak to me, invoking my many names. "Odin, Allfather," you might begin, or "Wanderer of the Nine Worlds, Keeper of Runes." Titles were important, for they shaped the connection. Call me by the name that suits your purpose, and you will find me listening. You would speak your request aloud, not timidly but with strength and clarity, for I do not hear whispers of hesitation.

If you sought wisdom, you would say so plainly. If you

sought strength in battle, you would not beg but pledge your valor in return for my aid. You might weave your words into poetry, for poetry is my language, the rhythm carrying your request to my ears with power and grace.

The Symbols

Runes were often carved or drawn to seal the ritual. You might mark *Ansuz* for wisdom, *Tiwaz* for victory, or *Algiz* for protection. These runes were not just marks; they were living energy, carried by your will. You would carve them into wood, stone, or even into the earth itself, leaving them as a sign of your intent.

The Silence and the Wait

After the words were spoken, there was silence. You would not demand my answer on the spot, for such arrogance is not fitting. Instead, you would wait, listening to the crackle of the fire, the rustle of the wind, the signs carried in the natural world. A raven's call, the shift of smoke, the stirring of the flame— these were my replies.

The Farewell

When the ritual was complete, you would thank me. Gratitude was never skipped, for it was as much a part of the exchange as the offering itself. You would extinguish the fire if it were safe to do so or leave it to burn down naturally, a final act of devotion.

The Result

And then you would leave, returning to your life, watchful for my answers. They might come in dreams, in sudden flashes of inspiration, or in the subtle unfolding of events. The old rituals were not about instant gratification; they were about aligning yourself with the forces that shape the world, trusting that the favor you asked would come in the way most fitting.

That is how I was called upon in the old days, with fire, offering, words, and unwavering intent. Those who approached me with respect found me willing to answer. Those who came with arrogance or empty hearts found only silence.

CHAPTER 3

Modern Magik with Odin

Now, let's bring all this into the modern world. It's the early decades of the Twenty-First century, few of us have access to animal skins, antlers, and the like.

In fact, working with Odin doesn't require elaborate ceremony, towering halls, or relics lost to time. His energy is vast, his wisdom boundless, but his methods are direct. He is a god of knowledge, war, leadership, and transformation—one who expects action, not endless preparation. When we work with Odin in modern magik, we strip down the ritual to what matters most: intent, offerings, and connection.

Traditional Norse magik was raw and practical, tied to the land and the needs of the moment. A warrior seeking victory would carve runes into his weapon. A skald looking for inspiration would drink mead and call on Odin through poetry. A chieftain needing wisdom would seek a vision, offering gifts in return for clarity. These methods remain as potent today as they were centuries ago. The only difference is that now, we tailor the practice to fit our modern lives.

Offerings

Odin is a god who values sacrifice, but not in the way many imagine. His idea of sacrifice isn't just about giving something up; it's about trading something of value for something greater. When working with Odin, the offerings should reflect respect, knowledge, and a willingness to engage with his power.

Beer, mead, whiskey, and scotch are all highly favored by Odin. Mead, the most traditional of these, holds deep significance because of the myth of the Mead of Poetry—stolen by Odin himself to grant wisdom and poetic inspiration to those worthy. Offering mead to Odin is a direct acknowledgment of his role as the seeker of knowledge, the drink itself acting as a bridge between the mortal mind and divine insight. If mead is unavailable, a strong beer, whiskey, or scotch serves just as well, all carrying that fire and depth Odin enjoys. The offering isn't about the price tag or rarity—it's about what it represents: a willingness to share something of value in exchange for knowledge, strength, or guidance.

When making the offering, it should be poured into a dedicated vessel, spoken over, and then either left outside for nature to claim or poured into the earth. The act of pouring symbolizes the transfer of energy between realms, a simple but effective way of bridging the gap between mortal and god.

Incense

Scent is one of the most primal triggers of memory and presence, a way of signaling to Odin that you are calling upon him. In the past, smoke from burning wood, herbs, or animal offerings carried prayers to the gods. Today, we use incense to create the same effect—clearing the space, signaling intent, and building the energetic connection to Odin's realm.

For Odin, the best incense choices are woods and resins with deep, earthy scents. Frankincense is an excellent choice, long associated with wisdom, divine communication, and ritual. I use frankincense often, so much so, that I purchase frankincense in one-pound (0.5 kgs) packages. If you wish to use stick incense, the best is one called "King of Frankincense". The seller has seemed to have disappeared, so do a search for one called "Hojary Frankincense Sticks" - which takes 2nd place.

Cedar and pine bring the energy of deep forests and Yggdrasil itself, reinforcing the connection to Odin's wisdom and world-spanning presence. I managed to locate a wonderful stick incense, but this brand has disappeared. Look for stick incense made in Tibet, if at all possible. Otherwise, locate Japanese made cedar incense. Honestly, incense companies seem to come and go, so when you find a favorite, stock up on it. Personally, using cedar incense triggers memories of growing up and having camp fires using cedar and juniper, and cooking over these fires.

Sandalwood, though not native to Norse lands, carries a grounding, ancient energy that aligns well with Odin's knowledge and authority. Myrrh, often paired with frankincense, adds a layer of transformation, making it ideal for rituals seeking deep wisdom or change.

If incense is unavailable, burning dried herbs such as rosemary or sage can work just as well. Both carry purifying properties and are easy to obtain. The smoke itself is what matters—it acts as a conduit, lifting the spoken words and energies to the divine.

Phrasing the Request

Odin does not respond well to weak or uncertain words. He is a god of knowledge, but also of action, and those who come to him must do so with a clear purpose. This is not a spirit that tolerates rambling or half-hearted requests. If you seek Odin's help, know what you want and state it directly.

When making a request, use strong, confident wording.

Instead of saying, *"Odin, I think I might need help deciding on my career,"* say, *"Odin, I seek your wisdom in choosing the best path for my future. Reveal what I must know."* The difference is subtle, but important. Odin responds to those who take charge of their own destiny, those who acknowledge that they must act once knowledge is given.

If you are performing a ritual, this request should be spoken aloud, preferably after meditation or visualization. Words carry power, and saying them with intent solidifies the energy of the request. It is also wise to write the request down, either carving it into wood, writing it on parchment, or using a rune associated with the request. This tangible act reinforces the connection between thought, action, and divine assistance.

Special Timings

I rarely advise on any special timings in any magik. I feel the magik you can bring forth is enough to make a desire manifest, however, some magik does require keeping an eye on the moon and days of the week. Timing can amplify the power of a ritual, aligning personal energy with greater cosmic forces. While Odin can be called upon at any time, there are certain days and lunar phases that strengthen the connection.

Wednesday is Odin's day—this is no coincidence, as the modern name stems from "Woden's Day," directly linking it to him. Performing rituals on a Wednesday enhances wisdom-seeking, decision-making, and personal growth, making it an ideal time for asking Odin for guidance or insight.

When working with the moon, the waxing (going from new to full) phase is best for drawing in knowledge, opportunities, and inspiration. The full moon amplifies all magik, making it the most potent time for any ritual calling upon Odin. The waning moon (after the full moon), while often used for banishing, can also be useful for seeking transformation, making it a powerful time for rituals where you ask Odin to remove obstacles or grant the strength to leave something behind.

If possible, working at dusk or dawn strengthens the connection, as Odin is a god of transitions—the meeting of night and day, the crossing of worlds, the shifting of fate. These liminal moments hold power, reflecting his nature as the one who walks between.

Colors

Color holds deep symbolic meaning in magik, and working with Odin is no exception. When setting up an altar or choosing candles and materials for a ritual, selecting the right colors can enhance the connection and focus the energy.

Gold represents wisdom, leadership, and divine knowledge. It is the color of enlightenment, making it perfect for rituals seeking Odin's guidance or insight. Green connects to prosperity and growth, suitable for those looking to expand in business, personal development, or creative endeavors. Deep blue aligns with Odin's connection to the vast cosmos, bringing in higher wisdom and spiritual insight. Black, while often associated with banishing, is also the color of mystery and the unknown, making it an excellent choice for rituals seeking hidden knowledge.

Using these colors can be as simple as choosing a candle in the right shade, placing cloth on an altar, or even wearing the color during the ritual. The visual presence reinforces the energy of the working, strengthening the intent and the connection.

Optional Items

The whole idea of an altar and special items on it that resonate with the ritual and spirit to be summoned is to create an atmosphere which signals commitment. Odin does not tolerate hesitation or half-hearted devotion. The way one prepares an altar speaks to their seriousness, their understanding of what they are asking, and their readiness to act when knowledge is granted.

A bare altar can be enough if the heart is fully engaged, but a carefully prepared one shows reverence, an acknowledgment of the weight of the request. It is a reminder that Odin is not simply called upon for entertainment or curiosity—his guidance changes lives, often through sacrifice and challenge.

The altar, then, becomes a place of focus, a sacred space

where distractions are left behind, and only purpose remains.

Odin doesn't demand a lavish altar, but here are some items you can include (and why) in your altar for ritual to The Allfather. Each of these items serves a purpose, a way to attune your energy to his, reinforcing the themes of wisdom, strength, and transformation that define his essence.

A Spear or Spear Symbol

Gungnir, Odin's legendary spear, never misses its mark. A small replica of a spear, a carved symbol of one, or even a simple wooden staff representing it can serve as a conduit for Odin's unwavering precision and ability to guide outcomes with unshakable certainty. If you seek clarity, purpose, or the ability to direct your energy toward a specific goal, placing a spear symbol on your altar is a powerful way to focus Odin's influence.

A Raven Feather or Raven Representation

Odin's ravens, Huginn and Muninn, represent thought and memory—two forces essential for wisdom and strategic thinking. A raven feather, a small carving, or even a printed image of ravens can act as a reminder to observe, to listen, and to interpret the signs around you. Those seeking knowledge, insight, or prophetic visions may find that incorporating the raven into their altar helps sharpen the mind and improve the perception of subtle messages. We have several huge ravens on this property, and I have received gifts from each of them. One found a golf ball and left it for me on this stump I use to leave them offerings. Where he found this golf ball is a mystery. Closest golf course is 15 miles (24 kilometers) distant.

A Small Mirror or Reflective Object

Odin sees far beyond the surface, into the past, the present, and even the winding paths of fate. A small mirror on the altar can symbolize his ability to reflect hidden truths, aiding in divination and self-discovery. Those performing rituals for insight into difficult situations, uncovering deception, or exploring their own subconscious will find this item enhances the ability to receive clear, unfiltered knowledge.

A Wolf Symbol or Representation

Geri and Freki, Odin's two wolves, embody hunger—both the literal hunger of survival and the spiritual hunger for knowledge and strength. A wolf image or figurine on the altar calls forth the drive to push forward, to sharpen instincts, and to embrace the challenges that forge power. This is particularly effective for those seeking strength in adversity, determination in career paths, or courage in personal trials.

Runes or a Carved Rune Stone

The runes are Odin's greatest gift to humanity, a direct link between the divine and mortal understanding. A single rune carved onto wood or stone—particularly Ansuz (for wisdom and communication), Raidho (for direction and guidance), or Tiwaz (for strength and victory)—can be placed on the altar to align the working with Odin's guidance. Those seeking wisdom through direct messages, either in dreams or signs, may find that focusing on a rune enhances their ability to receive and interpret Odin's answers. I have two runes (Tiwaz and Ansuz) I made myself, carving them into slices of wood from a downed birch tree.

A Cup or Drinking Horn

Odin is closely tied to mead, the drink of wisdom and poetry. A cup or drinking horn filled with mead, whiskey, or even water can be placed on the altar as both an offering and a representation of Odin's endless thirst for knowledge. This is particularly fitting for rituals asking for insight, creative inspiration, or leadership wisdom. If you sip from the cup after offering it, it can serve as a way to symbolically take in the wisdom you seek.

A Feather or Representation of Wind

Odin is a god who moves—between realms, between identities, between roles of war and wisdom. The wind carries knowledge, just as the breath carries words. A feather or an item that represents movement (a small wind chime, a fan, or even dried leaves) can be used on the altar to invite Odin's presence. This is useful for those looking for direction, whether in travel, career, or personal transformation.

A Key or Symbol of Unlocking

Odin does not hand out knowledge freely; it must be sought, unlocked, and earned. A key placed on the altar represents hidden wisdom waiting to be revealed. It is particularly useful for those working with Odin to uncover secrets, unlock new opportunities, or push past mental and spiritual barriers.

Bones or a Symbol of Death and Rebirth

Odin walks the line between life and death, often seeking knowledge from the dead, communing with spirits, and guiding warriors to Valhalla. A small, ethically sourced bone or an item symbolizing the cycle of death and rebirth (such as an antler shed naturally from a deer) acknowledges his connection to transformation. This is most useful for those undergoing major life changes, seeking to leave an old version of themselves behind, or embracing the wisdom that comes from endings. Please source these ethically.

Wood or Bark from a Strong Tree

Yggdrasil, the World Tree, binds all things together. A small piece of wood, particularly from a strong tree like oak, ash, or pine, ties the altar to Odin's role as the keeper of knowledge across the nine worlds. This serves as a grounding force, useful for rituals seeking stability, longevity, and deep-rooted wisdom.

Each of these items can be incorporated into an altar space when working with Odin, but none are strictly necessary. As always, it is not about the objects themselves but the intention behind their use. Some may choose a minimal altar, with only a candle and a small offering, while others may feel drawn to include several of these elements. The most important thing is that each item resonates with your purpose, creating a space where Odin's presence is not only invited but honored.

Bringing It All Together

Calling upon Odin today does not require a return to ancient times. Anyone who insists this magik can only be worked in the traditional methods is a gatekeeper and they need to step away from their prejudice.

Intent, gang. It's intent. The core of Odin's power is lies not in elaborate ceremonies, but in the intention, the offerings, and the directness of the request. With mead or whiskey, a candle in the right color, the scent of frankincense or cedar filling the air, and words spoken with purpose, Odin will hear you. The energy of his presence is sharp, guiding, and relentless—expect answers, expect shifts, and be ready to act when wisdom is given.

Rituals

The various rituals that follow are just a starting spot. I encourage you to experiment, alter rituals to fit your situation or desire, and make notes so that you know what changes you made, and what effect the changes caused.

For a basic ritual, there are only four key items you'll be needing. The candle for your desire, your written petition, some incense, and a rune that represents your desire. You should also have Odin's symbol (as a paper sigil, in the back of this book). That's it. Everything else is just stage dressing.

CHAPTER 4

Wisdom for Career Advancement and Decision-Making

Here, we'll call upon Odin to provide guidance in career-related matters, whether it's making an important decision, seeking new opportunities, or gaining insight into the best path forward. The approach is simple, using only the most effective elements to align with Odin's wisdom.

Items Needed:

- Altar candles (one white for wisdom, one gold for success)
- Sigil of Odin (back of the book, or a simple Ansuz rune drawn on paper)

- Incense (Frankincense or cedar for clarity and wisdom)
- Offering (Mead, whiskey, or beer)
- Offering vessel (A small cup or bowl)
- Petition (A written request describing the career issue or decision)
- Ritual candle for this purpose (Blue for wisdom, or gold for career success)
- A small stone or coin (To represent the tangible outcome of your career path)

Stand before your altar and take a deep breath. Visualize a boundary forming around your space, separating it from distractions and outside energies. If needed, run a quick banishing by waving your hand through the air and stating:

"All that does not serve my purpose is cast out. In this space, only wisdom remains."

Light the altar candles first, then the ritual candle. Let the scent of the incense fill the air, shifting the energy of the space.

Hold the stone or coin in your hands. Close your eyes and focus on the career decision or path ahead. Imagine the different outcomes and feel which one carries the strongest energy.

Hold the sigil or rune of Odin and speak with confidence:

"Odin, Allfather, guide my mind and sharpen my vision. Show me the path to success."

Pause for a moment, allowing his presence to settle.

Pick up your written request and read it out loud, speaking clearly and with intent. Hold the petition over the flame of the ritual candle for a few moments, allowing it to absorb your energy.

Sit quietly for a moment. Watch the candle's flame or close your eyes and remain open to any thoughts, images, or feelings that arise. Odin often communicates through subtle signs—trust that the answer will come.

Pour the mead, whiskey, or beer into the offering vessel and say:

"Odin, I give this in thanks. May my path be clear."

Leave the offering on the altar for 24 hours before pouring it into the earth.

Snuff out the candles, but let the ritual candle burn down naturally if possible. Place the stone or coin somewhere visible as a reminder of the wisdom received. Write down any thoughts or insights—Odin's guidance may come through dreams, conversations, or sudden realizations in the coming days.

After 24 hours, respectfully dispose of the offering outdoors, thanking Odin one final time.

This ritual creates the space for Odin's wisdom to reach you, but the answer won't always come immediately. Watch for signs, stay open to new perspectives, and trust your intuition. When the path becomes clear, act with confidence—Odin favors those who take bold steps forward.

CHAPTER 5

Windfall of Money

This ritual calls upon Odin's wisdom and influence to open pathways for unexpected financial gain. Whether it comes as an opportunity, a sudden gift, or an increase in business, this working aligns you with abundance in its most accessible form. The method is kept simple, focusing only on the most effective elements to call Odin's favor.

Items Needed

- Altar candles (one green for prosperity, one gold for fortune)
- Odin's Sigil (see appendix for sigil details) or a Fehu rune drawn on paper to represent wealth

- Incense (Sandalwood for success or cinnamon for financial luck)
- Offering (Mead, whiskey, or beer)
- Offering vessel (Cup or bowl)
- Petition (A written request for financial gain, clearly stating the need)
- Ritual candle (Gold for wealth or green for financial growth)
- A coin or small bill (To symbolize the money you seek)

Ritual Steps

Cast your circle, ensuring your space is free from distraction. Close your eyes, take a deep breath, and visualize yourself surrounded by the energy of abundance. If needed, perform a quick banishing to remove any stagnant or limiting energy:

"All obstacles are cleared, all blockages are lifted. Let the path of fortune open wide."

Light the altar candles first, followed by the ritual candle. Let the warm glow shift the energy in the room, signaling the start of the working. Place the incense on the burner, allowing its scent to rise, calling Odin's presence.

Hold the coin or bill in your hand, focusing on the wealth you seek. Imagine it multiplying, the energy of prosperity expanding outward, reaching every corner of your life. See money flowing in, unexpected yet perfectly timed, as Odin's influence weaves the threads of fate in your favor.

Pick up Odin's sigil or the Fehu rune and hold it as you speak the summoning:

"Odin, Allfather, Keeper of Fate, Open the way for wealth to flow, join with me in my space."

Pause for a moment, feeling the energy shift. If thoughts or images enter your mind, take note of them—they may be Odin's way of guiding you toward the right opportunities.

Read the petition aloud, stating your need with confidence and certainty. Pass it over the flame of the ritual candle, letting it absorb the power of the working. If you wish, place it under the coin as a physical anchor for your request.

Pour the offering into the vessel and raise it slightly, saying:

"Odin, I give this in gratitude. May wealth find its way to me."

Leave the offering on the altar for 24 hours before pouring it into the earth.

Snuff out the candles, allowing the ritual candle to burn down naturally if possible. Keep the coin or bill in a place where money is handled—your wallet, cash register, or business space—as a symbol of the wealth now moving toward you.

After 24 hours, respectfully dispose of the offering outdoors. Watch for unexpected opportunities, sudden insights, or fortunate events in the coming days—Odin's wealth often arrives in ways you don't expect, but it always arrives when you are ready to receive it.

CHAPTER 6

Finding Your Ideal Life Partner

Odin's deep understanding of fate and human nature makes him an excellent guide in aligning you with the right person. This ritual calls upon his wisdom to connect your path with that of a compatible life partner. It is a simple, direct working designed to clear obstacles, strengthen self-confidence, and invite the right energies into your life.

Items Needed

- Altar candles (one pink for love, one red for passion and attraction)
- Odin's Sigil (see appendix for this sigil)
- Incense (Rose for romance or frankincense for

divine guidance)

- Offering (Honey, symbolizing sweetness and harmonious connection)
- Offering vessel (A small dish or bowl)
- Petition (A written request describing the qualities of your ideal partner)
- Ritual candle (Pink or red, representing the love you seek)
- A small mirror (To reflect your own energy outward and attract love)

Ritual Steps

Cast your circle, centering yourself in the space. Take a deep breath, letting go of past disappointments or doubts. If you need to clear lingering emotional energy, run a quick banishing by stating:

"All barriers to love are dissolved. The path before me is open."

Light the altar candles, then the ritual candle. Let their glow shift the energy in the room, warming the space and signaling the start of the working. Place the incense on the burner, allowing its fragrance to rise and set the tone for love and connection.

Hold the small mirror in front of the candle's flame, gazing into it. See yourself not as you are, but as you wish to be—confident, radiant, and fully open to love. Envision the type of partner you seek, the qualities they hold, and the life you will build together. Let the image in the mirror reflect not only who you are, but the love that is already aligning with your fate.

Pick up Odin's sigil and hold it as you speak the summoning:

"Odin, Allfather, Keeper of Wyrd, Join with me and listen to my request."

Let the words settle into the space, knowing Odin hears and weaves the unseen threads of connection.

Read your petition aloud, speaking with certainty, as though you are calling love to you in this moment. If the wording feels off, change it—Odin values clarity and intent. Pass the petition over the candle flame briefly, charging it with the energy of the working. If desired, place it beneath the mirror to hold the energy of the ritual.

Pour the honey into the offering vessel, lifting it slightly as you say:

"Odin, I give this in thanks. May love come in its rightful time."

Leave the offering on the altar for 24 hours before placing it outdoors as a final act of gratitude.

Extinguish the candles, allowing the ritual candle to burn down naturally if possible. Keep the mirror somewhere visible to remind you of the love that is drawing closer each day.

After 24 hours, respectfully place the honey offering outside, preferably near flowers or trees, as a gift back to nature. Stay open to new connections and unexpected encounters— Odin's hand moves fate in ways that often surprise, but always guide toward what is truly meant to be.

CHAPTER 7

Strength and Perseverance to Start a Business

Odin's resilience and sharp strategic mind make him the perfect ally for those seeking to build something lasting. Whether you're starting a business, launching a new project, or pushing through obstacles in your career, this ritual calls upon Odin's strength and focus to ensure your efforts hit their mark. Simple yet effective, it aligns your will with his unwavering determination.

Items Needed

- Altar candles (one white for clarity, one gold for success)
- Odin's Sigil (see appendix for sigil details)

- Incense (Cedar for stability or frankincense for success)
- Offering (Mead, whiskey, or strong coffee as a symbol of focus and perseverance)
- Offering vessel (A small cup or bowl)
- Petition (A written business goal, clearly defined)
- Ritual candle (White for wisdom and focus)
- A small stone (Symbolizing the solid foundation of your business)

Ritual Steps

Cast your circle, setting the space for clear thought and unwavering focus. If distractions or doubt linger, take a deep breath and state:

"All obstacles are removed. My path is clear, my aim is true."

Light the altar candles, then the ritual candle, allowing their light to fill the space. As the flame flickers, let it represent the fire of creation, the spark that fuels your ambition. Place the incense on the burner, breathing in its scent as you center yourself in the moment.

Hold the stone in your hand, feeling its weight, its solidity. This is your foundation—your business, your vision, your future. As you focus on it, see your goal taking form, the pieces coming together, and success building upon itself. Place the stone before the candle, anchoring the energy of the working.

Pick up Odin's sigil and hold it as you speak the summoning:

"Odin, Allfather, relentless and wise, As Gungnir flies straight and true, fly to be with me in my space."

Let his presence settle around you, guiding your focus and resolve.

Read your business goal aloud, speaking as though it is already unfolding before you. See Odin's spear, Gungnir, flying toward the target—unerring, unstoppable. Visualize your goal manifesting with the same certainty. Hold the petition over the flame briefly, charging it with the energy of the working, then place it beneath the stone.

Pour the offering into the vessel, raising it slightly as you say:

"Odin, I offer this in gratitude. May my path be one of strength and success."

Leave the offering on the altar for 24 hours before pouring it into the earth as a final act of respect.

Snuff out the candles, allowing the ritual candle to burn down naturally if possible. Keep the stone in your workspace, on your desk, or wherever your business dealings take place, letting it serve as a lasting anchor of Odin's guidance.

After 24 hours, respectfully dispose of the offering outdoors, acknowledging that success is built not in a single moment but in sustained effort. Watch for signs, unexpected insights, or new opportunities—Odin's strength moves with those who act boldly and with purpose.

CHAPTER 8

Uncovering Hidden Opportunities

Odin's relentless pursuit of knowledge and his mastery over the unseen make him the perfect guide when seeking hidden opportunities. Whether it's a business prospect, a life-changing connection, or an overlooked path to success, this ritual calls upon Odin to lift the veil and reveal what has been obscured. This working is simple yet powerful, using only a few meaningful items to shift your perception and attune you to Odin's guidance.

Items Needed

- Altar candles (one silver for insight, one black for mystery and revelation)

- Odin's Sigil (see appendix for sigil details)
- Incense (Frankincense for wisdom or mugwort for heightened awareness)
- Offering (Mead, whiskey, or black coffee to fuel clarity and deep thought)
- Offering vessel (A small cup or bowl)
- Petition (A written request for guidance in uncovering hidden opportunities)
- Ritual candle (Silver for clarity or black for unveiling the unknown)
- A small reflective object (A coin or mirror to symbolize insight and reflection)
- A small pouch of herbs (Sage or rosemary for clarity and heightened perception)

Ritual Steps

Cast your circle, allowing your space to shift from the ordinary to the sacred. If doubt or hesitation lingers, clear it by stating:

"That which is hidden, now comes to light. That which is lost, now finds its way."

Light the altar candles, then the ritual candle. Watch the flames flicker, illuminating the unseen, creating a space where

Odin's knowledge flows freely. Place the incense on the burner, letting its smoke carry your intent beyond the limits of your conscious mind.

Hold the reflective object in your hands. This represents the vision you seek—the ability to see beyond what is obvious, to perceive the hidden paths Odin can reveal. Gaze into it, letting your mind open to possibilities you may not have considered. Let your thoughts drift, unbound by logic or expectation.

Pick up Odin's sigil and hold it as you speak the summoning:

"Odin, Allfather, Keeper of Secrets,
Lift the veil and reveal what lies unseen.
Guide my steps toward what awaits,
Let the hidden path be known."

Let the energy settle, allowing Odin's wisdom to take root.

Read your petition aloud, speaking with certainty, as if the hidden opportunity is already on its way to you. Pass the petition briefly over the ritual candle's flame, charging it with the working's energy, then place it beneath the reflective object.

Take the pouch of herbs and pass it over the flame of the

ritual candle, allowing the energy of the ritual to infuse it. As you do, say:

"Odin, with this, I carry your sight. Let me perceive the paths unknown."

Pour the offering into the vessel, lifting it slightly as you say:

"Odin, I offer this in gratitude. May your wisdom guide my steps."

Leave the offering on the altar for 24 hours before placing it outside as a final act of respect.

Extinguish the candles, allowing the ritual candle to burn down naturally if possible. Keep the reflective object in your space as a reminder to stay open to Odin's guidance. Carry the herb pouch with you for the next week, paying close attention to unexpected opportunities, conversations, or signs—Odin often reveals his answers in ways that require perception and action.

After 24 hours, respectfully place the offering outdoors. Hidden opportunities do not always appear in an instant, but they unfold when the mind is ready to recognize them. Be observant, take note of synchronicities, and act when the moment presents itself—Odin's wisdom is for those who seek and those who dare to follow the path once it is revealed.

CHAPTER 9

Connecting with Odin for Direct Guidance

There are times when books, divination, and signs are not enough—you need to hear directly from Odin. This ritual calls upon him as the Wanderer, the seeker of wisdom, the giver of knowledge. He does not always answer in words, but through images, sensations, and insights that arise when the mind is open. This is a simple working designed to create a moment of direct connection, where Odin's presence can be felt, and his guidance can be received.

Items Needed

- Altar candles (one gray for wisdom and mystery)
- Odin's Sigil (see appendix for sigil details)

- Incense (Cedar for clarity or myrrh for connection to divine wisdom)
- Offering (Mead or bread, symbols of nourishment and sacred exchange)
- Offering vessel (A small cup or plate)
- Ritual candle (Gray to reflect Odin's many aspects)
- A symbol of Odin (A raven figure, a small staff, or an item that personally connects you to him)

Ritual Steps

Cast your circle, shifting your awareness from the mundane to the sacred. If distractions linger, clear the space by stating:

"Only wisdom enters this space. I call upon the Wanderer, the Seeker, the One-Eyed God."

Light the altar candles, then the ritual candle. Watch the flame as it flickers, a beacon calling Odin forth. Place the incense on the burner, letting the scent rise, signaling the beginning of the connection.

Place the offering on the altar. Mead, if available, is best, as it ties directly to Odin's lore, but bread is equally powerful as a symbol of sustenance and exchange.

Hold Odin's symbol in your hands, feeling its weight, its energy. Let your mind open to his presence. Close your eyes if you wish, breathing deeply, settling into the moment.

Speak his name:

"Odin, Wanderer, Keeper of Runes, I seek your wisdom, your voice, your sight.

Join with me here, Show me what I must know."

Let the space grow quiet. Do not force thoughts, do not reach—simply allow. Pay attention to any images that arise, any thoughts that surface unbidden, any emotions that shift within you. Odin speaks in ways beyond words, and his presence is often felt rather than heard.

If an insight comes, acknowledge it. If nothing arrives immediately, trust that the message will come in the hours or days ahead—through dreams, sudden realizations, or unexpected encounters.

When you feel the moment is complete, lift the offering vessel slightly and say:

"Odin, I give this in gratitude. May wisdom flow freely between us."

Leave the offering on the altar for 24 hours before

placing it outside as a final act of respect.

Extinguish the candles, allowing the ritual candle to burn down naturally if possible. Keep Odin's symbol close in the coming days, as the connection formed here may continue to strengthen.

After 24 hours, respectfully dispose of the offering outdoors. Watch for Odin's presence in small details—a raven crossing your path, a phrase that lingers in your mind, a sudden knowing of what must be done. He is a god of answers, but also of questions, and those who seek his wisdom must be prepared to act when the path is revealed.

CHAPTER 10

Boosting or Creating New Income Streams

Odin's wisdom extends beyond battle and poetry—he is a master strategist, a seeker of knowledge, and a guide for those who wish to carve their own path. Whether you are looking to increase your current income or open the door to new financial opportunities, this ritual aligns your energy with Odin's ability to uncover wealth where others see none. With the simplest methods, this working clears obstacles, sharpens focus, and invites financial growth into your life.

Items Needed

- Altar candles (one gold for wealth, one green for financial growth)

- Odin's Sigil (see appendix for sigil details)
- Incense (Cinnamon for money attraction or sandalwood for success)
- Offering (Mead, whiskey, or a few coins as a token of prosperity)
- Offering vessel (A small cup or dish)
- Petition (A written request describing the income goal or opportunity you seek)
- Ritual candle (Gold for abundance, or green for financial stability)
- A small token representing money (A coin, business card, or even a folded bill)

Ritual Steps

Cast your circle, allowing the space to shift from limitation to possibility. If doubts or financial blocks linger, clear them by stating:

"Scarcity dissolves, and new wealth flows. My hands are open, my path is clear."

Light the altar candles, then the ritual candle, letting their glow set the tone for abundance. Place the incense on the burner, allowing its scent to carry the energy of prosperity into the air.

Hold Odin's sigil in your hands, feeling its presence.

Odin does not deliver wealth without effort—he illuminates the path, sharpens the mind, and brings the right opportunities forward. As you focus on the sigil, see doors opening, money flowing in, and new ventures emerging in unexpected ways.

Speak the summoning:

"Odin, Seeker of Knowledge, Weaver of Fate, Turn my eyes to the hidden streams of wealth."

Hold your petition in your hands and read it aloud, stating your financial goal with certainty. Pass the petition briefly over the flame of the ritual candle, charging it with the energy of success, then place it beneath the token representing money.

Pour the offering into the vessel and lift it slightly, saying:

"Odin, I give this in gratitude. May fortune flow as freely as wisdom."

Leave the offering on the altar for 24 hours before placing it outside as a final act of respect.

Extinguish the candles, allowing the ritual candle to burn down naturally if possible. Keep the money token in your wallet, at your workspace, or in a place tied to your financial efforts as a symbol of the wealth now moving toward you.

After 24 hours, respectfully dispose of the offering outdoors. Stay aware of new financial opportunities, sudden insights, and unexpected gains—Odin's favor works through action, and those who seek abundance must be ready to claim it when it appears.

CHAPTER 11

Pathworking Odin

Pathworking is a direct and powerful method of connecting with Odin, bypassing the need for physical tools or elaborate ritual. It serves as a bridge between your consciousness and his vast, dynamic presence, allowing you to share space with him in a realm of wisdom, transformation, and hidden knowledge. Unlike standard rituals, which rely on candles, incense, and spoken words to summon a spirit or deity, pathworking immerses you in Odin's energetic domain, aligning you with his essence in a way that is both deeply personal and profoundly transformative.

However, this is not something to take lightly. You are not merely imagining Odin—you are stepping into his current, his energy field, his mindscape. His presence is sharp, vast, and relentless. Those who approach him must do so with purpose and clarity, for his answers are rarely simple, and his influence can shift the way you think, act, and perceive the world.

Why Pathworking? A Ritual Replacement with Deeper Impact

For many, pathworking becomes a preferred method over traditional rituals. While physical rituals work by shaping external energies, pathworking reshapes you, bringing you into direct resonance with Odin's power. When you enter his presence, you absorb his energy, and this can change you in ways you may not fully realize at first.

Unlike a simple invocation where you request Odin's aid, pathworking places you within his space. You are not calling him to you; you are traveling to him. This creates a more immediate, unfiltered experience, where insights, messages, and transformations happen in real time. Odin will challenge your assumptions, press you to think beyond limitations, and push you toward self-discovery in ways that traditional ritual may not.

This method also works well for those who lack access to private ritual space, have restrictions on burning incense or candles, or simply prefer an internalized approach. It allows for direct spiritual contact in a quiet and controlled manner, accessible anytime and anywhere.

The Risks and Challenges of Pathworking with Odin

Stepping into Odin's space is not without its risks. He is not a soft, gentle deity who speaks in riddles designed to comfort you. He is a god of wisdom, but that wisdom is often earned through sacrifice, challenge, and deep personal reflection. When you engage in pathworking with Odin, you must be prepared for several key challenges:

Absorbing Odin's Energy Can Shift Your Mindset

His presence is intense, filled with a ceaseless hunger for knowledge, an unstoppable drive to push forward, and an understanding of sacrifice few can comprehend. Spending time in his space may change the way you think—expect sudden insights, a sharper mind, and an awareness of things that were once hidden to you. However, this can also make you restless, always seeking more, never satisfied with surface-level knowledge. If you are not ready for that kind of transformation, tread carefully.

Messages Are Not Always Immediate or Obvious

Odin rarely speaks in a straightforward manner. His guidance may come in the form of symbols, fragmented images, or even strange riddles. It is up to you to decipher them, and sometimes the meaning will only become clear days or weeks later. If you are someone who seeks immediate, clear answers, you must be patient.

Maintaining Focus Is Crucial

Pathworking requires deep concentration. If your mind is easily distracted, it can be difficult to maintain a strong connection with Odin's energy. Thoughts of daily worries, unfinished tasks, or random mental chatter can pull you out of the experience before it fully unfolds. To combat this, creating the right mental and physical conditions is key.

Preparing for Pathworking: Staying Focused and Alert

One of the best ways to prepare for deep pathworking is to bring your body into a relaxed but alert state. If you are too tense, you will struggle to enter a deep meditative space. If you are too relaxed, you may drift into daydreaming or even sleep. The key is to find the balance between physical calm and mental sharpness.

Herbal teas can assist with this, acting as a bridge between relaxation and heightened awareness. The right herbs will quiet the body while keeping the mind sharp and focused, allowing you to hold the pathworking space more effectively.

Some recommended herbal teas for this practice include:

•Mugwort – Known for its ability to enhance visions and dreams, mugwort is excellent for opening the mind to Odin's messages. However, it is strong and should be used in moderation.

- Peppermint – A simple but effective herb that clears the mind and increases alertness. Ideal for those who struggle with mental fog during meditation.
- Rosemary – A herb of memory and clarity, rosemary helps sharpen the mind, making it easier to recall details from your pathworking experience.
- Lemon Balm – Calming yet mildly stimulating, lemon balm keeps you relaxed without making you too drowsy.
- Ginseng or Green Tea – If you tend to lose focus or feel your mind drifting too much, a small amount of ginseng or green tea can provide gentle stimulation without overstimulating the body.

Drinking a cup of one of these teas about 20 minutes before pathworking can help set the right internal conditions for success.

Keeping a Journal: Recording Your Travels to Odin's Space

Pathworking is not a one-time event—it is a practice, a way to consistently deepen your relationship with Odin. Because of this, keeping a journal of your experiences is invaluable.

Each time you enter Odin's space, write down the details of what you saw, felt, and experienced as soon as you return to normal awareness. Even if something seems insignificant at the time, it may prove meaningful later.

Pay particular attention to:

- Any symbols or objects Odin gives you
- Specific words or phrases that come to mind during the pathworking
- Feelings or emotional shifts that occurred while in his presence
- Any animals or figures that appeared in the vision
- The environment around Odin—was it a forest? A battlefield? A storm? These elements can provide clues about the nature of his message

Many people find that reviewing their notes weeks or months later brings new insights they didn't catch at the time. Odin's wisdom often unfolds in layers, revealing itself gradually rather than all at once.

Final Thoughts: Walking Odin's Path

Pathworking with Odin is not a passive experience—it is an active, immersive way to align with his power and guidance. It is for those who seek knowledge and are willing to engage in deep personal reflection. Odin will not coddle, and he will not hand you easy answers. But if you step into his world with respect, purpose, and an open mind, he will show you things you never imagined possible.

Approach this practice with intent. Keep your mind

sharp, your focus steady, and your willingness to learn unshaken. Odin does not favor those who hesitate—he favors those who seek, act, and shape their own path.

Seeking the Allfather's Wisdom

Odin does not come to those who hesitate—he comes to those who seek. This pathworking is designed to create a direct connection to him, opening a space for his wisdom to reach you. There are no tools needed, only your focus and the willingness to receive what he has to offer.

Step 1: Preparing the Mind

Find a quiet space where you will not be disturbed. Sit comfortably, either in a chair with your feet on the ground or on the floor with your legs crossed. Close your eyes and take a slow breath in, then exhale completely. Let any tension drain from your body with each breath.

Continue breathing deeply and evenly, allowing your thoughts to settle. If distractions arise, acknowledge them and let them pass without attachment. You are preparing to step into Odin's presence, and the path must be clear.

Step 2: Entering the Journey

In your mind's eye, picture yourself standing at the edge

of a vast forest. The air is crisp, the scent of earth and pine filling your lungs. The towering trees stretch into the distance, forming a winding path ahead.

You take your first step forward. With each step, the sounds of the modern world fade, replaced by the rustling of leaves, the distant call of a raven, and the steady crunch of earth beneath your feet. You are walking toward knowledge, toward wisdom, toward the presence of the Allfather himself.

As you move deeper into the forest, you notice a figure in the distance. A lone traveler stands beside a great tree, cloaked in gray, a wide-brimmed hat casting a shadow over his face. He leans on a staff, watching as you approach.

This is Odin.

Step 3: The Meeting with Odin

You stop a few feet away, waiting. The air around him hums with something ancient, something powerful. He lifts his head slightly, and for the first time, you see his eye—one eye, sharp and knowing, piercing through you as if reading every thought you've ever had.

He does not speak first. He waits for you to state your purpose.

Take a moment to gather your thoughts. Why have you come? What question or guidance do you seek? When you are ready, say it aloud in your mind. Odin listens, considering your words with a nod.

He reaches into his cloak and produces something—a rune, a small object, a feather from one of his ravens. Whatever he gives you is symbolic, holding the answer you seek. Accept it and study it. The meaning may not be immediately clear, but trust that it will reveal itself in time.

Odin speaks now, but his words are not always straightforward. Sometimes he tells a story, sometimes he asks a question in return. Sometimes his answer is silence, a test to see if you already hold the wisdom you seek.

Listen.

Step 4: Returning with the Knowledge

Odin turns, stepping away from the tree, fading back into the shadows of the forest. The wind picks up slightly, rustling the branches above. You look down at what he has given you, memorizing every detail.

Slowly, you begin to walk back the way you came. The forest shifts, the sounds of the modern world creeping back in. Step by step, the vision fades.

Breathe deeply, bringing yourself back to your physical surroundings. Feel the surface beneath you, the air in your lungs. When you are ready, open your eyes.

Step 5: Reflect and Act

Sit for a moment and process what you experienced. Write down any symbols, words, or emotions that stood out to you. Odin's answers are often layered, requiring reflection and action to fully understand.

Look for signs in the coming days—messages in unexpected places, repeated symbols, or a sudden realization that connects to what you received. Odin does not simply hand out wisdom; he gives the tools to uncover it for yourself.

Use what you have learned. The path to Odin is not one of passive understanding—it is a path of action, growth, and transformation.

Universal Pathworking to Odin

This pathworking serves as a direct connection to Odin, allowing his wisdom, strength, and influence to flow into your life. Whether seeking knowledge, wealth, love, protection, or any of the other aspects covered in this chapter, this pathworking can replace or enhance any ritual by immersing you in Odin's presence. Unlike traditional invocation, this is not a request from afar—you are stepping into his space, allowing his energy to align with your intent.

This pathworking requires only Odin's sigil, your written petition, and the willingness to be fully present in the experience. Upon returning, an offering must be made as a sign of gratitude and respect, completing the exchange and sealing the connection.

Items Needed

- Odin's Sigil (see appendix for sigil details)
- Your Petition (A written statement of your request, clear and specific)
- A Small Offering (Mead, whiskey, bread, or coins to be given after the journey)

Step 1: Entering the Meditative State

Find a quiet place where you will not be disturbed. Sit comfortably, holding Odin's sigil in one hand and your petition in the other. Close your eyes and take a slow, deep breath in, then exhale completely. Repeat this process until your body relaxes, and your mind quiets.

Let go of the noise of daily life. If thoughts arise, acknowledge them, then let them drift away like smoke on the wind. You are stepping into a space where the Allfather's presence is strong, where the wisdom of the ages flows freely.

Step 2: The Journey to Odin's Realm

In your mind's eye, see yourself standing at the base of a great tree—Yggdrasil, the World Tree, its massive roots twisting into the earth, its branches stretching toward the heavens. The air is thick with energy, and you feel the pull of something unseen, something ancient.

Before you, a path emerges. You begin to walk, each step taking you deeper into the unseen, into the space where Odin waits. The surroundings shift as you move forward—forests, mountains, vast plains—all landscapes of memory, fate, and wisdom.

Ahead, a small fire burns, its embers glowing in the dim light. A figure sits beside it, draped in a gray cloak, a wide-brimmed hat casting a shadow over his face. He does not move, but you know he is waiting for you.

This is Odin.

Step 3: Presenting Your Request

You stop a few feet away, feeling the weight of his gaze even before he lifts his head. One eye, piercing and unyielding, locks onto yours. He studies you—not just your face, but everything beneath it. The thoughts you hold. The fears you suppress. The purpose that has brought you here.

Holding his sigil and your petition firmly, you take a deep breath and state your request. Speak clearly, directly, with confidence. Do not beg, do not hesitate—Odin respects those who know their desires and are willing to pursue them. If you do not know what to say, simply state:

"Odin, Allfather, I seek your guidance. Show me what I must know. Lead me where I must go."

He listens. There is no impatience in his posture, only the weight of timeless understanding.

Step 4: Receiving Odin's Guidance

Odin's answers do not always come in words. Sometimes, he speaks in symbols—a rune appearing in the flames, a shape forming in the shadows. Other times, he gives an object, something simple yet significant. He may gesture for you to follow him, leading you through an experience that will serve as your answer.

Trust what unfolds. Do not force the vision to fit your expectations. Odin shows what you need, not necessarily what you want. Pay close attention to details—the landscape, the sounds, any sudden emotions. Everything carries meaning.

If he speaks, listen carefully. His words are rarely straightforward, but they will linger in your mind long after this journey ends. If he remains silent, the message may come later— through dreams, signs, or realizations in the days ahead.

When the vision begins to fade, acknowledge what you have received, even if its meaning is not yet clear.

Step 5: Returning and Sealing the Connection

Odin rises, his form beginning to blur, his presence pulling away. The fire dims, the world around you begins to shift. Step back, feeling the energy of the journey recede as you move away from the fire, away from the path, returning to where you began.

Slowly, bring your awareness back to the physical world. Feel the surface beneath you, the air in your lungs. When you are ready, open your eyes.

Take a few moments to sit in silence, absorbing the experience. If you received a symbol, a word, or a message, write it down immediately. Odin's wisdom often unfolds in layers— what seems unclear now may become obvious later.

Step 6: Offering and Gratitude

Odin does not work for free. He is a god of exchange, and wisdom always comes at a price.

Take the offering you prepared—mead, whiskey, bread, or coins—and place it outside, in nature. As you do, say:

"Odin, I give this in gratitude. May the wisdom you have shared guide my path."

Leave it there, undisturbed, as a final act of respect.

Final Thoughts: Watching for Signs

Odin's answers often appear in unexpected ways. A random phrase in conversation, a book that catches your attention, a raven appearing at the right moment—these are not coincidences. Pay attention to patterns, to repeated symbols, to sudden shifts in thought or perception.

Review your journal regularly. Write down anything significant that occurs in the coming days. Odin's guidance does not always arrive in a single moment; sometimes, it unfolds gradually, leading you where you need to go step by step.

This pathworking can be used for any request in this chapter, whether seeking prosperity, strength, love, or hidden knowledge. Each time you step into Odin's space, you deepen your connection with him, aligning yourself further with his power.

Walk with purpose. Act with confidence. And remember—when Odin shows you the path, it is up to you to take the first step.

PART TWO

THOR

CHAPTER 12

Thor: The Thunderer, The Protector, The Unyielding Force

Thor's name echoes through time, a force as undeniable as the storms he commands. He is more than just a warrior god, more than the slayer of giants—he is the shield of Midgard, the guardian of humanity, and the embodiment of unrelenting strength. Where Odin is the seeker of hidden wisdom, weaving fate's threads through sacrifice and cunning, Thor is the unshakable wall, standing between chaos and order, ensuring that the world remains whole. He is the god of action, of immediate results, of power that does not hesitate.

For centuries, he was the most beloved of the Norse gods. While kings and warlords sought Odin's guidance, it was Thor who watched over the farmers, the craftsmen, and those who toiled to build their lives in an unforgiving world. He is the god of storms, yes, but also of protection, stability, and perseverance—the kind of power that does not falter under pressure but instead grows stronger in adversity.

It is impossible to separate Thor from Mjölnir, his mighty hammer. A weapon forged by the dwarves, Mjölnir is more than just a tool of destruction—it is a symbol of divine authority, a force that keeps the balance of existence intact. When it crashes down, it is not just a blow struck against an enemy, but an affirmation that chaos will never reign unchecked. In this way, Thor is not merely a god of battle—he is a cosmic force, ensuring that the world does not collapse into disorder.

Thor is often seen as straightforward, even simple compared to the more enigmatic Odin. But to dismiss him as just a brute with a hammer is to misunderstand his nature. Thor's strength is not mindless; it is focused, deliberate, and unwavering. He does not hesitate when action is needed. He does not overthink when instinct will do. This is why he remains so powerful—because sometimes, thought and hesitation are nothing compared to the force of sheer will.

To work with Thor is to align yourself with that power. He does not demand endless study or cryptic sacrifices—he asks for boldness, for determination, for an honest heart. If you seek his aid, you must be willing to stand firm, to push through obstacles, to take the action necessary to claim what is yours. He is not a god of waiting—he is a god of doing.

This section of the book is dedicated to Thor's magik—how to call upon his strength, his protection, and his ability to clear obstacles from your path. Whether you seek courage, success, or the resilience to weather life's storms, Thor's presence can be a driving force in your magikal practice. His power is immediate, his influence undeniable, and his lessons are as timeless as the storms themselves.

If you are ready to work with Thor, be prepared. He does not entertain weakness, nor does he grant favors to those who hesitate. Stand strong, speak clearly, and act with conviction. The Thunderer does not whisper—he roars. And if you are willing to listen, his power will shake the very foundations of your life.

Thor: The God vs. The Pop Culture Icon

In modern times, Thor's name has become almost as famous as it was in the age of the Vikings. Thanks to blockbuster movies and TV shows, he has been reimagined for a new audience, depicted as a heroic, noble warrior with a larger-than-life presence. But as with all things adapted for entertainment, the Thor of pop culture is a shadow of the true deity—a simplified, softened version of the Thunderer, stripped of his raw, primal force and reshaped to fit a narrative more palatable for modern audiences.

Thor in Myth vs. Thor in Movies and TV

The Marvel Comics version of Thor, brought to the screen in the Marvel Cinematic Universe (MCU), is perhaps the most recognizable interpretation of the god today. Played by Chris Hemsworth, this Thor is a powerful, charismatic warrior with a blend of arrogance, charm, and nobility. He wields Mjölnir, speaks in grandiose phrases, and often wrestles with his responsibilities as a god and prince of Asgard. While entertaining, this portrayal is, at best, a loose adaptation of the Thor of Norse mythology.

In the myths, Thor is not a golden-haired, Shakespearean-speaking noble with a neatly trimmed beard. He is a red-haired, fierce, and sometimes reckless god, known for his deep laugh, massive appetite, and boundless energy. He is a warrior first and foremost, but not in the polished way modern media depicts him—Thor is raw, aggressive, and deeply connected to the earth and the people of Midgard. His power does not come from his royal birthright but from his unshakable will, his ability to throw himself into battle without hesitation, and his refusal to let chaos or deceit stand unchallenged.

The Personality Shift: Noble Warrior vs. Protective Force of Nature

In movies, Thor is often portrayed as a noble hero on a

quest for self-discovery. The MCU takes this further by giving him a character arc that revolves around maturity, responsibility, and personal loss. He is flawed but ultimately well-intentioned, sometimes played for comedy, sometimes struggling with his place in the cosmos.

The true Thor of Norse belief is not on a journey of self-discovery. He does not hesitate or second-guess himself—his power lies in his certainty. He knows who he is, what he stands for, and what must be done. He does not need to "learn humility" or struggle with his role in the world. He is a god of action, not reflection.

Thor's true nature is protective, not introspective. He does not wander between worlds seeking enlightenment as Odin does; he exists to shield Midgard from the forces of destruction. His battles are not about personal growth but about maintaining order and keeping chaos at bay. This is why he is so beloved by farmers, warriors, and everyday people—he is not a distant, aloof god, but a force they can count on when the storm clouds gather.

Mjölnir: Weapon of War vs. Symbol of Cosmic Order

In modern adaptations, Thor's hammer, Mjölnir, is treated primarily as a weapon, a powerful tool that grants him the ability to control lightning and smash enemies. In the MCU, it has the additional feature of determining "worthiness," allowing only those pure of heart and noble in intent to lift it. While this makes for compelling storytelling, it is not entirely in line with the mythological Thor.

The true Mjölnir is not a judge of character—it is a divine force, a weapon of absolute power. Forged by the dwarves, it is not just a tool for combat but a sacred object, used in rituals, blessings, and protection. In Norse belief, Mjölnir was used to hallow marriages, consecrate land, and ward off evil forces. It was a symbol of Thor's divine authority and his role in maintaining the balance of the cosmos.

Additionally, the real Mjölnir is described as having a short handle, due to a mishap in its forging. Unlike the sleek, balanced hammer of the movies, Mjölnir in myth is a brutal, compact weapon, designed to crush its enemies with devastating force.

Thor's Relationships: The Mythic Family vs. Hollywood Adaptations

In pop culture, Thor's most famous relationship is with Loki, his adoptive brother and rival. The MCU plays up their dynamic as a mix of love, resentment, and betrayal, turning their interactions into a long-running character arc filled with conflict and redemption. While the relationship is entertaining, it is largely a fabrication of modern storytelling.

In Norse myth, Thor and Loki do share many adventures, but they are not brothers, nor do they have a deep emotional connection. Their dynamic is more akin to that of a reckless trickster and an exasperated warrior forced to clean up the mess. Loki's mischief often places the gods in danger, and while Thor accompanies him on many journeys, he is more often than not the one forced to set things right. There is no deep familial bond—if anything, Thor is one of Loki's greatest threats, as he is among the gods most likely to strike him down when his treachery is revealed.

Thor's most important relationship in the myths is with Sif, his wife, and his children, Magni, Modi, and Thrud. Sif is rarely explored in modern adaptations, but in myth, she is associated with the earth and fertility, and her golden hair symbolizes the ripening fields of wheat. Thor's role as a husband and father speaks to his nature as a protector, not just of the gods but of the world and his own kin.

The Final Fate of Thor: The Last Battle vs. The Ongoing Franchise

One of the most significant differences between mythological Thor and his pop culture counterpart is how their stories end. In the MCU, Thor's journey is ongoing, with each new film giving him new challenges to face. He is immortal in the way that superheroes are—always returning, always evolving, always setting up the next adventure.

The real Thor, however, has an ending. In Ragnarök, the

great final battle, Thor faces the serpent Jörmungandr, his greatest enemy. He slays the serpent, but not before it poisons him. Staggering only a few steps before succumbing, Thor dies, fulfilling his role as Midgard's greatest protector. He does not live to see the world rebuilt—his sacrifice ensures that the cycle of existence continues, but he himself is lost in the process.

This is one of the greatest aspects of Thor's mythology: his strength is not endless, but it is absolute. He gives everything, even his life, in the battle to preserve order. This is a fundamental departure from the Hollywood version, where Thor will always return for another fight. The real Thor does not get a sequel—his story ends with his final act of heroism.

To work with Thor in magik, one must understand him in his true form. He is not concerned with image or glory—he is a god of doing, of standing strong in the face of adversity, of fighting until the last breath. If you seek his power, be prepared to wield it as he would—with determination, with courage, and without hesitation.

CHAPTER 13

The Mythology of Thor: Son of the Storm, Guardian of the World

Thor's legend is one of might, thunder, and relentless protection. He is the strongest of the gods, the bulwark against chaos, the roaring storm that drowns out destruction. Yet beneath the crashing thunder lies a god who is more than just a warrior— Thor is a guardian, a champion of both gods and men, and a force that does not falter when the world is at stake. His myths are filled with battle, trickery, and divine strength, but they also reveal something deeper—a god who does not rule from a throne but walks among those he protects, striking down threats with his unstoppable hammer, Mjölnir.

Origins of the Thunderer

Thor's origins, like many Norse myths, come to us in pieces, scattered through the Poetic Edda and Prose Edda, compiled centuries after the old gods were last worshiped. His father is Odin, the enigmatic Allfather, god of wisdom, war, and fate. His mother is Jord, the personification of the earth itself. This parentage is no accident—Thor is the union of sky and land, the force that connects the heavens to Midgard, where humans dwell. He is both above and among the people, a bridge between cosmic power and earthly strength.

Unlike Odin, who relies on strategy, cunning, and long-reaching plans, Thor is direct. He does not scheme—he acts. And he acts with force that cannot be denied. He is not concerned with hidden knowledge or the twisting fate of the cosmos; he is concerned with now—with crushing enemies, with defending Midgard, with maintaining order in a world that teeters on the edge of destruction.

From the moment of his birth, Thor was different. As an infant, he was said to be so strong that even lifting him required great effort. As a child, he was wild and uncontainable, testing his strength against anything he could find, forever seeking a challenge worthy of him. This drive would carry through his life—Thor never stops, never hesitates, never doubts.

Thor's Mythological Family

Thor's family is vast, though often overshadowed by his own larger-than-life presence. His wife is Sif, a goddess of the earth, fertility, and abundance. She is known for her golden hair, a symbol of ripe fields of grain, making their union one of both storm and harvest—his power brings the rain, her presence ensures the land flourishes.

Loki, the trickster god, is not his brother, despite modern interpretations, but he is a frequent companion in Thor's myths—usually as the cause of some great trouble that Thor must then solve. Their dynamic is not one of familial love but of reluctant partnership, a collision of order and chaos.

Thor has several children, but the most well-known are Magni and Modi, whose names mean "Mighty" and "Brave." They are prophesied to survive Ragnarok, inheriting their father's strength and continuing his legacy when the old world falls. His daughter, Thrud, whose name means "Strength," is less spoken of in the myths but, fittingly, is associated with raw power like her father.

But for all his family connections, Thor is often depicted alone, standing against the forces of destruction with only Mjölnir in hand.

The Power of Thor: The Hammer, The Belt, and The Gloves

Thor's strength is legendary, but it is not his alone—it is

reinforced by three sacred tools that make him an unparalleled force.

First, there is Mjölnir, his hammer, forged by the dwarves Brokkr and Sindri. It is said that due to Loki's interference during its creation, the handle was made too short, requiring Thor to wield it one-handed. But despite this flaw, it is the most powerful weapon in existence, capable of leveling mountains, summoning storms, and destroying any foe, be they giant or god. Mjölnir is also a tool of consecration, used to bless marriages, hallow land, and ensure divine protection.

Thor also wears Megingjörð, the Belt of Strength, which doubles his already godly power. And finally, he dons the iron gloves, Járngreipr, which allow him to grasp Mjölnir fully and direct its immense force. With these three, Thor is unmatched. There is no trick, no deception—just sheer, unrelenting might.

Thor's Magik in Action: The Tale of the Giant Slayer

Thor's greatest battles are against the jötnar, the giants—primordial forces of chaos that threaten the balance of the worlds. He has fought countless foes, but one story captures his essence perfectly—the tale of Hrungnir, the stone-headed giant.

Hrungnir, the strongest of the jötnar, once boasted that he was mightier than Thor himself. Fueled by arrogance, he rode his steed Gullfaxi to Asgard and drank among the gods, declaring that he could smash Valhalla and throw Odin himself into Hel's realm. The gods, unwilling to start a battle within their own halls, allowed him to speak, but Thor would not stand for it.

When Thor arrived and saw Hrungnir boasting, he issued a challenge: the giant would face him in a duel. Hrungnir, caught in his own pride, agreed. He went to Jotunheim, calling for the strongest weapon the giants could forge—a massive stone shield and a whetstone to use as an axe.

The duel was set. Thor, arriving with Mjölnir, wasted no time. He hurled his hammer as Hrungnir threw his whetstone. The two weapons met in midair with such force that the whetstone shattered into pieces, raining down onto the land below. One shard struck Thor's head, wounding him, but Mjölnir did not stop. It smashed through Hrungnir's shield, then crushed his skull with such force that his own massive body collapsed under the weight of his destruction.

The battle was over in moments.

Thor, however, was trapped beneath Hrungnir's massive leg. No god could move it—only his young son, Magni, barely a child, was able to lift it from his father. Even in victory, Thor's legacy was already passing to the next generation.

This is Thor's power: decisive, unstoppable, undeniable. When faced with arrogance, he destroys it. When challenged, he does not hesitate. When chaos threatens, he answers with force that cannot be ignored.

Thor is not a god of trickery or half-measures. He does

not weave complex fates or whisper cryptic wisdom. His magik is one of immediate action, of sheer force, of protection that does not ask but commands. His myths are filled with stories of strength, but they are also stories of loyalty, protection, and the unshakable will to stand against the forces of destruction.

To call upon Thor is to call upon a god who acts. There is no waiting, no patience—only the hammer's strike, the crash of thunder, and the knowledge that no matter the threat, no matter the storm, Thor will stand.

Chapter 14

The Magik of Thor

I'll quickly cover the magik of Thor here, then expand on the magik in the rituals section.

Thor's power is raw, immediate, and unwavering. Unlike Odin, who operates through wisdom and strategy, Thor's magik is about force—both in battle and in everyday life. When calling upon Thor, expect magik that demands action, that requires you to meet his power with your own will. He does not grant favor to those who wait; he empowers those who are ready to stand up and seize what is theirs.

Strength and Endurance

Thor is best at this magik because he is the embodiment

of unyielding strength. He does not tire, he does not falter, and he never backs down, no matter how overwhelming the opposition. His endurance allows him to battle the giants, lift impossible weights, and wield Mjölnir with devastating force. When working with Thor for strength, expect to feel his presence like an unshakable force pressing against you, demanding that you push forward.

In ritual: Expect a surge of raw energy, a moment where your own doubts feel insignificant compared to the power you are calling upon. This magik is for those who need to carry heavy burdens, whether physical, emotional, or spiritual.

Protection and Warding

Thor is the guardian of Midgard, the shield between chaos and order. No enemy, no dark force, no trickery of Loki or giants can bypass his vigilance. His magik is not subtle—it is a wall, a barrier of pure force that nothing unwanted can pass through. When calling upon Thor for protection, you are calling upon a god who destroys threats rather than simply deflecting them.

In ritual: Feel the energy of Mjölnir itself—a protective strike that eliminates danger rather than just repelling it. This magik is for warding homes, driving away harmful spirits, and standing strong against personal attacks.

Breaking Obstacles

Thor does not ask for permission. If something stands in his way, it is broken. This is not a god of patience or diplomacy—this is a god of unstoppable force. If you have been stuck, if something refuses to move, if doors remain shut no matter how hard you push, Thor's power will shatter the barrier.

In ritual: The energy here is sudden, forceful, and final. Expect results that feel like a dam breaking—where there was once resistance, there is now an open road. This is for people ready to remove the obstacles in their path, even if it means radical change.

Justice and Fairness

Thor is a god of righteous anger, of setting wrongs right. He does not tolerate deception, corruption, or unfair treatment. If you have been wronged, if injustice has gone unchecked, calling on Thor brings swift, direct action. He does not seek revenge—he restores balance. The guilty are struck down, and fairness is restored.

In ritual: This energy is like a hammer crashing onto an anvil—deliberate, purposeful, unyielding. Expect justice to manifest quickly, often in ways that leave no doubt that Thor's hand is at work.

Fertility and Prosperity

Though known as a warrior, Thor is also a god of fertility and abundance. His role as a protector extends to the land itself—his storms bring rain, his strength ensures the cycle of life continues. His connection to the earth makes him an excellent deity for fertility magik, whether for growing crops, conceiving children, or fostering creative energy.

In ritual: Thor's fertility magik is grounded, physical, and full of life. It is not about subtle influence—it is about undeniable results. Expect a strong, grounded energy that reinforces growth, creation, and expansion.

Money Magik

Thor's power over wealth is tied to his strength and protection. He does not grant easy money—he grants the ability to earn, to fight for what is yours, to seize opportunities when they arise. His magik does not attract gold from nowhere, but it removes blockages, clears paths, and brings the opportunities needed to thrive.

In ritual: This is not passive attraction magik—this is action-driven wealth magik. Expect sudden opportunities, a burst of motivation, and the ability to create wealth through effort and determination. If you want money handed to you, look elsewhere. If you are ready to claim what is yours, Thor will stand with you.

Thor's magik does not favor hesitation. When you call upon him, be ready to act, to seize what is given, and to move forward without fear. He is a god of action, not waiting, and his power rewards those who are willing to meet him with strength and courage.

Thor's Magik Today

Thor's presence is not bound to the past. His power is as accessible today as it was when Viking warriors carved his name into their weapons and farmers called upon him for protection against storms. While his traditional offerings and symbols remain powerful, modern magik adapts Thor's influence to fit today's needs—financial success, career advancement, legal protection, and personal strength.

Thor's energy is straightforward, unwavering, and forceful. When calling upon him, your magik should reflect that. He does not respond well to hesitation, vague requests, or unnecessary embellishments. This is a god who acts—there is no subtlety in his thunder, no deception in his strikes. Whether seeking prosperity, protection, or the removal of obstacles, your rituals should be clear, direct, and full of intent.

Offerings to Thor: What He Prefers and Why

Thor is a god who values effort and sincerity. His offerings reflect that—strong drinks, hearty food, and symbols of resilience. When giving to Thor, you are not simply leaving gifts; you are engaging in an exchange, showing respect, and forging a bond.

Alcoholic Offerings: Strength and Honor

Thor has always been closely tied to fermented drinks, particularly those with bold, unfiltered flavors. These offerings hold deep significance, representing strength, endurance, and celebration.

- Mead (Honey Wine) – The most traditional offering, closely tied to Norse culture. Mead symbolizes honor, vitality, and divine connection. It was considered sacred, often used in feasts and oaths.
- Beer – A common and accessible offering, beer connects Thor to the people. Farmers and warriors alike drank beer in his name, and it serves as a down-to-earth yet deeply respectful gift.
- Whiskey and Scotch – These drinks embody strength and intensity. Aged, powerful, and full-bodied, whiskey is an ideal offering when asking for Thor's unwavering strength or when facing great challenges.

The best way to give these offerings is to pour them into the earth, symbolizing a return of energy. If indoors, they can be placed in a dedicated vessel on the altar and left for 24 hours before disposal outside.

Food Offerings: Nourishment and Power

- Thor is a god of physicality, deeply tied to nourishment and the sustenance of life. Offering food, particularly hearty and filling fare, aligns with his energy.
- Bread – Represents sustenance and stability, ensuring continued strength.
- Roasted Meat – If a more traditional offering is desired, cooked meats can be given, though vegetarian offerings are also accepted if done with sincerity.
- Apples – Connected to vitality and longevity, apples are an excellent offering for long-term endurance and success.

Food offerings should be left outside for nature to take, never discarded disrespectfully.

Incense for Thor: Scents That Carry Power

Scent is a powerful way to attune a ritual to Thor's energy. The right incense can amplify intention, creating a space that resonates with his presence. Thor's scents should be strong, grounding, and natural—earthy, fiery, or reminiscent of storm-charged air.

- •Cedar – Represents strength, grounding, and resilience. Perfect for protection and stability magik.
- •Sandalwood – A scent of power and endurance, used when seeking strength and perseverance.
- •Frankincense – A sacred resin that connects to divine authority and victory. Ideal for rituals of justice, protection, and overcoming obstacles.
- •Cinnamon – A fiery, energetic scent that fuels action and movement. Excellent for money magik, success, and breaking through barriers.
- •Pine – Symbolic of Thor's connection to Midgard and nature, pine is useful for grounding and protection.

Incense should be lit at the start of the ritual and allowed to burn throughout, carrying the intent of the working into the air.

Phrasing the Request: How to Speak to Thor

Thor responds to clear, bold requests. He does not entertain overly poetic or vague words—he is a god of direct action, and your petitions should reflect that. There is no need for excessive formalities, but there is a need for confidence.

A good request to Thor should:

- State exactly what you want – No rambling, no uncertainty. Be precise.
- Acknowledge that action is required – Thor does not give freely; he grants strength to those willing to act.
- Be spoken with conviction – Speak as though you expect an answer, not as though you are hoping for one.

Example Requests:

- *"Thor, lend me your strength. Let my body and mind be unshaken. Let me stand firm and push forward, no matter the storm."*
- *"Thor, remove all obstacles in my path. Smash through all that holds me back, and let the way be open!"*
- *"Thor, I call upon your power. Let my wealth grow, let my hands be steady, and let my success be unstoppable."*

If writing a petition, keep it just as strong and focused. Simple statements are best: "I will achieve financial success with Thor's power behind me."

Special Timings: Aligning Your Rituals with Thor's Energy

While Thor's energy can be called upon at any time,

certain days and lunar phases amplify his power. Timing your rituals to these moments strengthens your connection and increases effectiveness.

Best Days for Thor's Magik

- Thursday ("Thor's Day") – The best day for any ritual involving Thor. A day of power, action, and overcoming challenges.
- Tuesday – A secondary day for strength, victory, and battle-related magik.
- Saturday – A good day for protection and endurance work, as it reinforces stability.

Moon Phases for Thor's Magik

- Waxing Moon – Best for increasing strength, wealth, and prosperity.
- Full Moon – A time of heightened power, excellent for major workings involving Thor's strength or justice.
- Waning Moon – Ideal for breaking obstacles, removing enemies, and clearing negative influences.

If a ritual is tied to storms, working during a thunderstorm adds significant power, aligning with Thor's dominion over lightning and thunder.

Colors for Thor's Magik: Visual Energy Alignment

Using the right colors in candles, altar cloths, or ritual tools strengthens the connection to Thor's energy.

- Red – Power, strength, raw energy. Use for endurance and battle magik.
- Gold – Wealth, success, divine favor. Use for prosperity and financial growth.
- Green – Stability, prosperity, and fertility. Use for grounding and abundance.
- Blue – Justice, truth, and divine authority. Use when calling on Thor for fairness.
- Black – Warding, protection, and breaking barriers. Use when removing obstacles or shielding from harm.

Candles in these colors can be used to reinforce the intent of a ritual, while altar cloths or symbols painted in these colors act as long-term energy anchors.

If you cannot find any of these colors, simply use white.

Thor's magik is not about waiting—it is about doing. When working with him, be ready to act, to seize opportunities, and to meet his power with your own strength. He will not simply hand you what you ask for, but he will give you the endurance, courage, and force to take it for yourself.

Approach him with confidence. Offer sincerely. Speak with conviction. Then, follow through with action.

Thor does not favor those who hesitate. He favors those who move.

CHAPTER 15

Strength and Endurance

Thor is the embodiment of unstoppable strength, both physical and mental. He does not falter, does not yield, and does not break under pressure. This ritual calls upon his power to fortify your body, mind, and spirit—whether you need the endurance to push through a difficult time, the physical energy to meet challenges, or the mental resilience to stay firm in your path.

Items Needed

- Altar candles (one red for raw power, one gold for divine strength)
- Thor's Sigil (see appendix for sigil details)

- Incense (Cedar for fortitude or sandalwood for resilience)
- Offering (Beer, mead, or whiskey—symbols of endurance and warrior's strength)
- Offering vessel (A small cup or dish)
- Petition (A written statement of your need for strength and endurance)
- Ritual candle (Red for sheer energy or black for overcoming adversity)

Ritual Steps

Cast your circle, grounding yourself in the moment. Breathe deeply and center your focus on the strength you seek. If you feel drained or uncertain, push those thoughts aside—this is the space where Thor's power reigns. If needed, clear the space with a firm statement:

"Weakness has no place here. Only strength remains."

Light the altar candles, then the ritual candle. Watch the flames rise, growing stronger with each breath. Place the incense on the burner, allowing its scent to fill the space, reinforcing your intent.

Hold Thor's sigil in your hand, letting its energy build. This is the key to his power—his presence, his force. Feel the weight of it, the strength behind it.

Speak the summoning:

"Thor, lend me your might, that I may stand unshaken."

Hold your petition in your hands and read it aloud, speaking with absolute certainty. This is not a request—it is a statement of intent. You are not asking Thor to give you strength; you are calling on his power to awaken it within you. Pass the petition briefly over the flame of the ritual candle, charging it with the force of the working, then place it beneath the sigil.

Pour the offering into the vessel and lift it slightly, saying:

"Thor, I offer this in gratitude. May my strength match the force of the storm."

Leave the offering on the altar for 24 hours before placing it outside as a final act of respect.

Extinguish the candles, allowing the ritual candle to burn down naturally if possible. Keep Thor's sigil close in the coming days, as his strength does not fade—it remains, building within you, waiting to be called upon again.

After 24 hours, respectfully dispose of the offering

outdoors. Strength is not a momentary thing—it is built, reinforced, and claimed. Walk forward with the knowledge that Thor's power is now part of you, and no obstacle will stand unchallenged.

CHAPTER 16

Protection and Warding

Thor is the guardian of Midgard, the unbreakable shield against chaos and destruction. His power does not merely deflect threats—it obliterates them. This ritual calls upon his strength to create a protective barrier around you, your home, or those you wish to shield. Whether facing negative energy, spiritual attacks, or general misfortune, Thor's presence ensures that no harm will cross the line you set.

Items Needed

- Altar candles (one black for absorbing negative energy, one red for protective strength)
- Thor's Sigil (see appendix for sigil details)

- Incense (Frankincense for spiritual protection or cedar for strength and grounding)
- Offering (Beer, mead, or whiskey—symbols of Thor's warrior's oath)
- Offering vessel (A small cup or dish)
- Petition (A written statement of who or what you are protecting)
- Ritual candle (White for purity and protection, or blue for Thor's guiding force)

Ritual Steps

Cast your circle, declaring the space as sacred and unbreakable. If unwanted energies are present, banish them with a firm voice:

"All that would bring harm is cast out. This space is sealed in Thor's name."

Light the altar candles, then the ritual candle. Feel their light forming a boundary, a shield that extends beyond the physical. Place the incense on the burner, letting the smoke rise like a barrier, reinforcing your intent.

Hold Thor's sigil in your hand, focusing on his role as the protector of gods and men. Let his energy settle around you, like the weight of a great shield.

Speak the summoning:

"Thor, stand guard and let no harm pass."

Hold your petition in your hands and read it aloud. Be clear in your intent—define exactly what or who is being protected. Pass the petition briefly over the flame of the ritual candle, charging it with the energy of the working, then place it beneath the sigil.

Pour the offering into the vessel and lift it slightly, saying:

"Thor, I offer this in gratitude. Let your shield be strong around me."

Leave the offering on the altar for 24 hours before placing it outside as a final act of respect.

Extinguish the candles, allowing the ritual candle to burn down naturally if possible. Keep Thor's sigil near the protected space or carry it with you if the protection is personal.

After 24 hours, respectfully dispose of the offering outdoors. Trust that Thor's shield remains—unbreakable, unwavering, and ever-present. No force, seen or unseen, will cross it without being struck down.

CHAPTER 17

Breaking Obstacles

Thor does not negotiate with barriers—he crushes them. His power is raw, direct, and unstoppable. Whether you face a personal struggle, a financial setback, or an unseen force blocking your path, this ritual calls upon Thor's strength to obliterate whatever stands in your way. Expect movement, expect change, and be ready to step through the opening once the obstacle is gone.

Items Needed

- Altar candles (one red for force, one black for destruction of obstacles)
- Thor's Sigil (see appendix for sigil details)

- Incense (Dragon's blood for power or pine for Thor's strength)
- Offering (Beer, mead, or whiskey—symbols of unstoppable will)
- Offering vessel (A small cup or dish)
- Petition (A written statement describing the obstacle you wish to destroy)
- Ritual candle (Gold for victory or red for raw energy)

Ritual Steps

Cast your circle, clearing away hesitation, doubt, and fear. If the obstacle feels overwhelming, strike your fist against the altar or floor and say:

"Nothing stands before the might of Thor. This block shall fall."

Light the altar candles, then the ritual candle. Watch the flames rise, visualizing them burning through whatever stands in your way. Place the incense on the burner, letting the smoke carry your intent into the unseen.

Hold Thor's sigil in your hand, feeling the weight of Mjölnir behind it. See the obstacle in your mind—not as an unmovable wall, but as something already breaking apart, already falling away.

Speak the summoning:

"Thor, strike down this barrier and clear my path."

Hold your petition in your hands and read it aloud. Speak with certainty—what was once a block is now rubble. Pass the petition briefly over the flame of the ritual candle, charging it with the force of the working, then place it beneath the sigil.

Pour the offering into the vessel and lift it slightly, saying:

"Thor, I offer this in gratitude. Let no wall stand before me."

Leave the offering on the altar for 24 hours before placing it outside as a final act of respect.

Extinguish the candles, allowing the ritual candle to burn down naturally if possible. Keep Thor's sigil near you as a reminder that obstacles exist only to be shattered.

After 24 hours, respectfully dispose of the offering outdoors. Be ready—Thor does not remove barriers gently. Expect sudden changes, expect swift movement, and when the path is open, step forward with the strength to claim what is yours.

CHAPTER 18

Justice and Fairness

Thor does not tolerate deception, corruption, or wrongdoing. He is a god of action, a force that rights wrongs and delivers justice with swift, undeniable force. If you have been wronged, treated unfairly, or need justice to prevail, this ritual calls upon Thor's power to restore balance and set things right. His justice is not slow—it is immediate, clear, and inescapable.

Items Needed

- Altar candles (one blue for truth, one red for righteous strength)
- Thor's Sigil (see appendix for sigil details)
- Incense (Frankincense for divine authority or myrrh

for truth and justice)

- Offering (Beer, mead, or whiskey—symbols of Thor's unwavering judgment)
- Offering vessel (A small cup or dish)
- Petition (A written statement describing the injustice and the fairness you seek)
- Ritual candle (White for truth or gold for victory)

Ritual Steps

Cast your circle, clearing away doubt, fear, and deception. Stand tall, grounding yourself in the truth of your cause. If you seek justice, speak it aloud:

"Truth shall not be hidden. Justice shall not be denied. Thor's hammer strikes for the righteous."

Light the altar candles, then the ritual candle. See the flames as beacons of truth, burning away falsehoods and restoring balance. Place the incense on the burner, letting the smoke rise, carrying your cause into the unseen.

Hold Thor's sigil in your hand, feeling the weight of Mjölnir behind it. Let his presence settle around you, heavy with purpose and unshakable resolve.

Speak the summoning:

"Thor, let justice be done, and let truth stand

unchallenged."

Hold your petition in your hands and read it aloud, declaring the injustice and the fairness you seek. Pass the petition briefly over the flame of the ritual candle, charging it with the energy of the working, then place it beneath the sigil.

Pour the offering into the vessel and lift it slightly, saying:

"Thor, I offer this in gratitude. Let truth and fairness reign."

Leave the offering on the altar for 24 hours before placing it outside as a final act of respect.

Extinguish the candles, allowing the ritual candle to burn down naturally if possible. Keep Thor's sigil near you as a symbol of justice in motion.

After 24 hours, respectfully dispose of the offering outdoors. Justice may come quickly or through unfolding events, but once Thor's hammer has struck, there is no reversing its force. Be ready for truth to be revealed, wrongs to be corrected, and fairness to be restored.

CHAPTER 19

Fertility and Prosperity

Thor is not only the god of storms and battle—he is also the bringer of rain, the force that nourishes the land and ensures abundance. His power fuels growth, whether in crops, wealth, family, or personal success. This ritual calls upon Thor to strengthen fertility, increase prosperity, and bring lasting abundance into your life.

Items Needed

- Altar candles (one green for growth, one gold for prosperity)
- Thor's Sigil (see appendix for sigil details)
- Incense (Cedar for vitality or sandalwood for

abundance)

•Offering (Beer, mead, or bread—symbols of nourishment and Thor's blessings)

•Offering vessel (A small cup or dish)

•Petition (A written statement of the fertility or prosperity you seek)

•Ritual candle (Green for abundance or orange for success and vitality)

Ritual Steps

Cast your circle, grounding yourself in the energy of growth and abundance. If you feel blocked or lacking, clear the space with a strong declaration:

"Thor, let life flourish, let wealth flow, let abundance reign."

Light the altar candles, then the ritual candle. Feel their warmth as the energy of expansion, drawing prosperity toward you. Place the incense on the burner, letting the scent fill the space with the essence of growth.

Hold Thor's sigil in your hand, connecting to his strength and the force of creation that drives all things forward.

Speak the summoning:

"Thor, bring your blessings of growth and prosperity into

my life."

Hold your petition in your hands and read it aloud, stating your desire with clarity and confidence. Pass the petition briefly over the flame of the ritual candle, charging it with the energy of the working, then place it beneath the sigil.

Pour the offering into the vessel and lift it slightly, saying:

"Thor, I offer this in gratitude. Let prosperity and life take root."

Leave the offering on the altar for 24 hours before placing it outside as a final act of respect.

Extinguish the candles, allowing the ritual candle to burn down naturally if possible. Keep Thor's sigil in a place of importance—near your finances for prosperity, in a sacred space for fertility, or anywhere that symbolizes growth.

After 24 hours, respectfully dispose of the offering outdoors. Thor's energy moves swiftly—expect fertility, success, and abundance to take shape, as long as you are ready to claim and nurture the blessings he sends.

CHAPTER 20

Money Magik

Thor is not a god of idle fortune—his wealth magik is earned, seized, and defended. He does not simply attract gold; he clears obstacles, strengthens resolve, and opens paths to financial growth. This ritual calls upon Thor to bring wealth through action, courage, and determination, ensuring that prosperity flows steadily into your life.

Items Needed

- Altar candles (one gold for wealth, one green for financial stability)
- Thor's Sigil (see appendix for sigil details)
- Incense (Cinnamon for money attraction or frankincense

for success)

- Offering (Beer, mead, or whiskey—symbols of Thor's warrior's prosperity)
- Offering vessel (A small cup or dish)
- Petition (A written statement of your financial goal)
- Ritual candle (Gold for success, or orange for financial motivation)

Ritual Steps

Cast your circle, clearing away hesitation and doubt. If financial struggles have weighed on you, push that energy out with a firm declaration:

"Wealth flows to me. All obstacles to prosperity are shattered by Thor's power."

Light the altar candles, then the ritual candle. Watch their flames as symbols of growing wealth, burning away scarcity and limitation. Place the incense on the burner, allowing the scent to rise, carrying your financial intent into the unseen.

Hold Thor's sigil in your hand, feeling his force as a god who breaks through financial stagnation. Let his energy fortify your will to claim what is yours.

Speak the summoning:

"Thor, clear my path to wealth and let fortune be strong

in my hands."

Hold your petition in your hands and read it aloud, stating your financial goal as though it is already happening. Pass the petition briefly over the flame of the ritual candle, charging it with the energy of success, then place it beneath the sigil.

Pour the offering into the vessel and lift it slightly, saying:

"Thor, I offer this in gratitude. May my wealth be earned, held, and protected."

Leave the offering on the altar for 24 hours before placing it outside as a final act of respect.

Extinguish the candles, allowing the ritual candle to burn down naturally if possible. Keep Thor's sigil near your financial dealings—your wallet, bank records, business space, or anywhere tied to prosperity.

After 24 hours, respectfully dispose of the offering outdoors. Watch for new financial opportunities, sudden insights, or shifts in circumstances—Thor does not give wealth passively, but he will open the doors for those ready to seize them.

CHAPTER 21

Pathworking Thor

Pathworking is not just visualization—it is a method of direct immersion into the presence of a deity, aligning yourself with their force, their mindset, and their power. When you enter Thor's space, you are not just calling on him for aid—you are stepping into the storm, standing beside him as he wields Mjölnir, feeling the raw force of his presence as if you were standing in the heart of a thunderclap. This is not something to take lightly. Thor's energy is immediate, heavy, and full of momentum. If Odin's space is filled with deep knowledge and whispers of hidden wisdom, Thor's is charged with action, movement, and the undeniable weight of his strength.

Unlike other forms of ritual or invocation, pathworking

allows you to experience Thor directly, unfiltered. It does not require external tools, but it does require focus, presence, and the ability to handle the force of his energy once it moves through you. Thor does not do anything in half-measures. If you step into his presence, expect movement, expect change, expect power that does not ask if you are ready—it assumes you are, and it expects you to act accordingly.

What to Expect When Pathworking with Thor

The first thing to understand about stepping into Thor's energetic space is that he is a god of force, endurance, and direct action. If you are looking for slow, gradual change, you are in the wrong place. His presence is a push, a momentum that will either carry you forward or knock you flat if you resist it. Unlike Odin, who tests your mind, Thor tests your will.

This means that when you work with him in pathworking, you must be clear on your intentions. If you are uncertain, if you hesitate, the energy will feel overwhelming. It is not that Thor will harm you, but that his force is so great that standing in it unprepared is like facing a storm without shelter—you will be drenched, tossed, and shaken. If you are ready, however, you will find yourself filled with a confidence and clarity that is undeniable.

One thing to be cautious of is overexertion. Thor's energy is tied to movement, action, and endurance, and it is easy to get caught up in his momentum. Many who work with him describe a sudden, almost overwhelming urge to get up and do something—whether that means tackling a project they've been avoiding, charging headfirst into a challenge, or physically exerting themselves in some way. This is a great boost when properly harnessed, but if ungrounded, it can lead to burnout. It is vital to balance Thor's energy, channeling it purposefully rather than letting it consume you in a burst of unchecked effort.

Preparing for Pathworking: Staying Grounded and Alert

Because Thor's presence is so strong, maintaining focus is crucial. The moment your mind starts to drift, you risk losing your connection to the experience or, worse, coming out of it feeling unfocused and restless. Unlike with Odin, where drifting thoughts can sometimes bring unexpected wisdom, Thor's space requires full engagement.

One of the best ways to prepare is to bring your body into a state of relaxed readiness—not sluggish, not wired, but balanced. Herbal teas can help with this, acting as a bridge between physical relaxation and mental clarity. The right herbs will calm your body while keeping your mind sharp, ensuring that you stay present in the pathworking experience.

Some excellent herbal choices include:

- Ginger – Warming and energizing without

overstimulation, ginger aligns with Thor's fiery, active presence and keeps the body engaged.

- Peppermint – Clears the mind and refreshes the senses, helping maintain sharp focus.
- Rosemary – A powerful herb for memory and clarity, making it ideal for processing what you experience during pathworking.
- Ginseng – A natural energy booster, useful for keeping your mind alert without jitteriness.
- Nettle – Grounds excess energy and supports physical resilience, aligning well with Thor's endurance.

Drinking a cup of one of these teas 15–20 minutes before pathworking helps ensure that you enter Thor's presence with a clear mind and an alert body, ready to engage fully with the experience.

Keeping a Journal: Recording Your Travels to Thor's Space

Thor is not a god of riddles or slow revelations, but that does not mean his lessons are always immediate. When working with him, you may receive a burst of insight, an instinctive push toward action, or a sudden realization that only makes sense after the fact. This is why keeping a journal of your experiences is essential. Write your experiences down, folks. Only way to track your progress.

Each time you enter Thor's space, write down everything as soon as you return to normal awareness. Even if it seems minor, it may hold meaning later.

Pay attention to:

- Physical sensations – Did you feel an increase in energy? A sudden urge to move? A sensation of warmth or pressure? Thor's presence often manifests physically.

- Visual imagery – Unlike Odin's vast, cosmic visions, Thor's messages often come in bold, direct symbols—a hammer striking, a storm approaching, a path suddenly clearing.

- Words or commands – Thor is blunt. If he speaks, it will likely be short, direct, and absolute. There is no guesswork—he tells you what must be done.

- Emotional responses – Did you feel a surge of courage? A need to stand your ground? An overwhelming sense of determination? Thor's energy often works through emotions, reinforcing your willpower.

Review your journal regularly. Sometimes, a message that seemed unimportant at the time will reveal itself later. If you start seeing patterns, that is Thor guiding you toward something—whether it be a challenge to overcome, a path to take, or a truth to acknowledge.

This spirit doesn't do things halfway. If you step into his energy, be ready to act. He does not offer endless contemplation, nor does he test you with illusions. He shows you exactly what needs to be done, then expects you to do it. If you enter pathworking with him and receive a message, take it seriously. Hesitation is not something he respects.

Approach him with confidence, purpose, and readiness. Drink your tea, still your mind, and when you step into his presence, be prepared to hold your ground. If you are uncertain, he will make you certain. If you are weak, he will demand that you become strong. If you are lost, he will hand you a direction and expect you to follow it.

This is the power of pathworking with Thor—it is not just an experience, it is a shift in momentum. Once you enter his space, you do not leave as you were. You leave stronger, clearer, and ready to face whatever stands in your way.

Pathworking 1: Standing in the Storm

This pathworking is a direct experience of Thor's presence, placing you in his space where his energy can be felt and understood. There are no tools required—only focus, intent, and the willingness to stand before the god of thunder and strength. This is a practice of action, movement, and force. Thor does not whisper—he roars, and his power is not gentle. Be prepared for an experience that is immediate, clear, and leaves no room for hesitation.

Step 1: Entering the State of Readiness

Find a quiet place where you will not be disturbed. Sit with your feet planted firmly on the ground, your hands resting comfortably, either on your knees or in your lap. Close your eyes and take a deep breath in through your nose, holding for a moment before exhaling through your mouth.

Continue breathing steadily, allowing tension to leave your body. With each breath, let your awareness shift from the mundane world around you to the space within. You are preparing to walk into the presence of Thor—your body should be strong, your mind clear, and your will unshaken.

Step 2: Walking the Storm's Path

In your mind's eye, see yourself standing at the edge of a vast, open landscape. The sky above is dark, rolling with heavy storm clouds. The air is charged with energy, thick with the scent of rain, the promise of thunder vibrating in the distance.

A path stretches before you, rough and uneven, cutting through the open land. The wind picks up as you take your first step forward, the ground firm beneath your feet. Each step brings you closer to the heart of the storm. You are not afraid. You are meant to walk this path.

The wind howls, pushing against you, but you do not falter. The ground rumbles beneath your feet, but you do not stop. You feel stronger, more alive with every step. The air itself hums with power, and you know you are drawing closer.

Step 3: Meeting Thor

Ahead, through the flashing storm, you see a figure standing on a high ridge. He is massive, unmoving, his presence undeniable. His red beard catches the flickering lightning, his broad shoulders seem as unshakable as the mountains. He holds Mjölnir in one hand, resting it easily at his side, as though it weighs nothing.

As you approach, the ground beneath you quiets. The wind no longer fights you—it bows to his presence.

Thor watches you, one piercing gaze fixed on you, his stance unrelenting. He does not speak first—he waits.

This is the moment where you declare your purpose. Say what you need, not in weakness, not as a plea, but with certainty. Why have you come? What strength do you seek? What force must be unleashed in your life?

Speak your words with power, knowing that Thor respects only those who are willing to act.

Step 4: Receiving Thor's Strength

Thor does not waste time with riddles or empty promises. His response may come in one of many ways.

He may nod in acknowledgment, his presence alone filling you with the strength you need.

He may raise Mjölnir, and in that moment, you feel an unshakable force enter you, igniting something dormant within.

He may gesture toward the storm, and in the distance, lightning strikes the earth, showing you that no obstacle is unbreakable.

Trust what you feel, what you see, what you hear. Thor's message will not be hidden. It will be clear, direct, and undeniable.

Step 5: Returning with Thor's Power

The storm does not fade—it moves with you. As you turn to leave, you are no longer the same. The power that filled the sky now moves within you.

Step by step, you walk away from the ridge, back along the path, feeling charged, certain, unshaken. The storm does not vanish—it follows, not as a threat, but as a force now connected to you.

With each step, the sounds of the wind fade. The weight of the vision begins to shift. The physical world calls you back.

Breathe deeply. Feel the ground beneath you. Wiggle your fingers, your toes. Slowly, when ready, open your eyes.

Step 6: Carrying Thor's Strength Forward

Thor does not grant strength for it to be wasted. The energy you have taken from this pathworking must be used. Do something with it.

If you asked for courage, act boldly.

If you sought endurance, push forward.

If you needed obstacles removed, start breaking them down.

Step 7: Offering

Thor does not ask for endless tributes, but he does demand respect. His aid is not given freely—it is an exchange.

Take a small offering—mead, beer, whiskey, or bread—and place it outside in nature. As you leave it, say:

"Thor, I give this in gratitude. May my strength match the storms you bring."

Walk away without hesitation. The exchange is complete.

Write down what you experienced, especially any symbols, words, or emotions that stood out. Thor's power does not linger in hesitation—it moves. Carry his presence forward in action, in strength, and in certainty.

Pathworking 2, Speaking Your Petition to the

Thunderer

This pathworking places you directly in the presence of Thor, where you will speak your petition with confidence and receive his strength, guidance, or force to break through obstacles. There are no physical tools needed—only your petition, your voice, and the willingness to act once Thor answers.

Thor does not favor hesitation or uncertainty. When you enter his space, you must be clear in your intent. This is not a god who deals in riddles or slow contemplation—he grants momentum, action, and power. Speak with conviction, knowing that you are stepping before the Thunderer himself.

Step 1: Entering the State of Readiness

Find a quiet space where you will not be disturbed. Sit with your feet planted firmly on the ground, your spine straight. Hold your petition in both hands, feeling the weight of your words, knowing they will be carried to Thor himself.

Close your eyes and take a deep breath in, filling your lungs completely. Hold for a moment, then exhale fully. Repeat this until your mind is steady, focused, and present. With each breath, let distractions fade. Your purpose is clear.

Step 2: Walking to the Storm's Edge

In your mind's eye, see yourself standing on a long,

winding path. The land around you is vast and open, the sky heavy with dark storm clouds rolling above. The air is charged, thick with the scent of rain, the distant growl of thunder vibrating in your chest.

You walk forward, each step firm and steady. The wind pushes against you, but you do not slow. You know where you are going. You belong here.

Ahead, a mighty figure stands—broad-shouldered, unshaken by the storm. His red beard moves slightly in the wind, but his stance is strong, immovable. He grips Mjölnir in one hand, resting it lightly as though it carries no weight, though you know it could shatter mountains with a single strike.

This is Thor. He watches you approach, his gaze sharp, expectant. He does not call you forward—you were already coming.

Step 3: Reading Your Petition

You stand before him, your petition in hand. His presence is undeniable, filling the space with energy that crackles like distant lightning. He waits, silent, expectant.

Take a breath. Read your petition aloud. Speak with certainty, knowing that your words do not fall into empty air. You are speaking to the god of storms, of action, of raw power.

Say your request clearly. Whether it is for strength, protection, justice, prosperity, or courage, speak as though you already believe in its fulfillment. Do not beg. Do not hesitate. Thor respects those who stand firm in their words.

As you speak, feel the storm around you shift. The wind changes, the clouds roll faster, a distant crack of thunder rumbles across the sky. Thor has heard you.

Step 4: Receiving Thor's Response

Thor does not always answer in words, but his response is always felt.

You may see lightning strike the earth, a sign of action, a command to move forward immediately.

You may feel a surge of energy in your chest, the weight of hesitation breaking apart.

You may sense a nod of approval, a simple but undeniable confirmation that your petition has been acknowledged.

Whatever the sign, trust it. Thor does not deal in uncertainty. His answers are clear, powerful, and absolute.

Step 5: Returning with Thor's Power

You nod in respect, knowing that what was asked is now in motion. You turn from Thor and begin walking back down the path. But you are not the same. The storm does not fade—it follows, inside you, moving through your blood, your muscles, your will.

With each step, the thunder softens, the energy around you settles. The path becomes clearer, the ground beneath your feet solid and sure.

Breathe deeply. Feel the air in your lungs, the new power in your body. Slowly, when ready, open your eyes.

Step 6: Giving an Offering

Thor does not ask for endless tributes, but he does demand respect. His aid is not given freely—it is an exchange.

Take a small offering—mead, beer, whiskey, or bread—and place it outside in nature. As you leave it, say:

"Thor, I give this in gratitude. May my strength match the storms you bring."

Walk away without hesitation. The exchange is complete.

Final Thoughts: Act, Do Not Wait

Thor's power is about action. Once you have walked this path, you must act. If you asked for courage, step forward. If you asked for protection, trust in the shield that has been given. If you asked for obstacles to be broken, strike first before they strike you.

Thor does not favor those who hesitate. He answers those who move. Now, move forward.

APPENDIX

Odin Sigil

Sigil for Odin

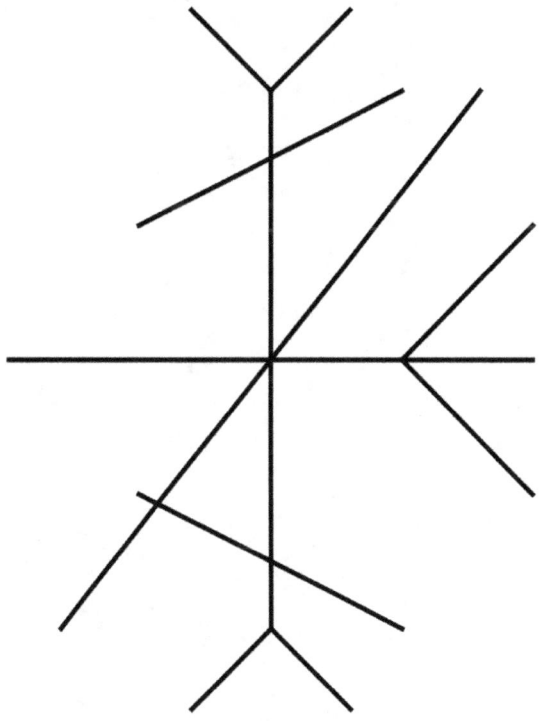

Thor Sigil

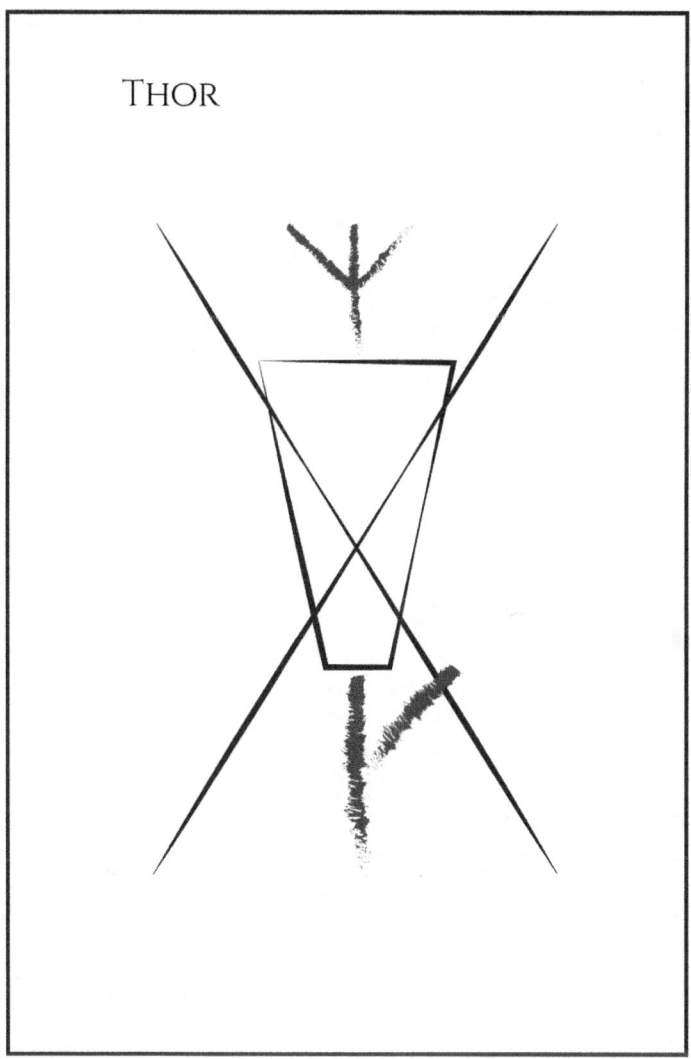

ABOUT THE AUTHOR

Dave is an author of adult fantasy (The Furies series) as well as author of occult books about magick. Dave has multiple advanced degrees in the occult, including a Doctorate in Literature, plus Doctor Honoris causa in Ancient Religions, Doctor Honoris causa in Demonology, Doctor Honoris causa in Divinity, Doctor Honoris causa in Magik.

He began working ritual magik back in the 1970s. He took a brief break, then used the power of this magik to create a photography career which took him to Los Angeles and work as a photographer for multiple magazines.

Dave has studied magik in all forms, and in 2018, released a three-part magik instruction course in High Magik. Thousands of students have benefited from David's unique teaching style, making ceremonial magik accessible to everyone.

Dave also has a series on Grecian Magick, exploring the aspects of ceremonial magick with the gods and goddesses of ancient Greece.

Magik Books by David Thompson

Available as EPUB, Paperback and Hardcover (*)

High Magick Series
- High Magick 101
- Daemons of High Magick
- Daemons and the Law of Attraction*
- Magick of Astaroth*
- Hidden in Plain Sight
- Lilith: Goddess of Darkness and Light*
- Daemons of Fortune*
- Asmodeus King of Daemons*
- Goddesses of High Magick
- Protection Magik
- The Diviner's Handbook
- The Magik of Lucifer*
- The Magik of Freya and Frigg
- The Magik of Sorath
- Goddesses of Vengeance
- Magik of Genius Spirits
- Power of Pathworking

Grecian Magick Series
- Magick of Apollo

- Magick of Hermes
- Magick of Aphrodite
- Magick of Fortuna*
- Greco-Roman Wealth Magick*
- Magick of the Sirens/Magick of the Muses
- Hermes and the Akashic Records

Magik for Everyone Series
- Candle Magik for Everyone
- Magik of Love & Lust

Fiction Novels by David Thompson

The Furies Series
- Angels of Vengeance
- Descent into Tartarus
- Furies: Beginnings
- Brianna: Making of a Fury

To connect with Dave, you can check his website at https://davepsychic.com

Social media links are at https://davepsychic.com/social-media-links/

www.ingramcontent.com/pod-product-compliance
Lightning Source LLC
Chambersburg PA
CBHW071746120626

46550CB00002B/679